The Lucky Ace Of France

BY

Jacques Mortane
And
R.L. Sherer

Copyright 2012
By R.L. Sherer

No part of this book may be reproduced in any form or by any electronic or mechanical means including information storage and retrieval systems, without permission in writing from the copyright owner. The only exception is by a reviewer, who may quote short excerpts in a review.

PREFACE	5
FOREWARD	6
CHAPTER II	17
CHAPTER III	23
CHAPTER IV	27
CHAPTER V	31
CHAPTER VI	37
CHAPTER VII	47
CHAPTER VIII	53
CHAPTER IX	57
CHAPTER X	61
CHAPTER XI	65
CHAPTER XII	69
CHAPTER XIII	77
CHAPTER XIV	83
CHAPTER XV	89
CHAPTER XVI	91
CHAPTER XVII	97
CHAPTER XVIII	103
CHAPTER XIX	107
CHAPTER XX	113
CHAPTER XXI	119
CHAPTER XXII	123
CHAPTER XXIII	127
CHAPTER XXIV	133
CHAPTER XXV	139

CHAPTER XXVI 145
CHAPTER XXVII 153
CHAPTER XXVIII 163
CHAPTER XXIX 171
CHAPTER XXX 179
CHAPTER XXXI 187
APPENDIX 199
THE PHOTOGRAPHIC LIBRARY OF CAPTAIN GEORGES GUYNEMER 217

PREFACE

In the pages which I shall consecrate to the glorious hero of whom France is so proud, my aim will be to make him known just as he was in the aerodromes. It is the fighter, the master of technique whom we study in one.

I shall add not a phrase to what the Ace of Aces was willing to confide to me in the conversations held with him. He agreed to tell me of his pursuits and to give me his opinions, while I took notes scrupulously, writing at his dictation. I did not trust my memory, leaving to Guynemer's own words all of their flavor.

My part was limited to being rather a faithful secretary to him who consented to speak to me about his profession with open soul. He knew my veneration for all that had to do with the "Fifth Arm," remembering that the first article devoted to "Sergeant Guynemer" had been written by me. And these several reasons had formed a bond of sympathy between us of which I am very proud.

FOREWARD
Advice To Boche Hunters

By
Captain Georges Guynemer

The public as a rule has a false idea of hunting and the hunters. They very easily imagine that we are way up there at our ease, directing events, and that the nearer we are to heaven the more we are invested with Divine Power. It is the duty of the journalists to educate their readers and prevent them from cherishing opinions as wrong as they are pitiable.

I cannot express in words the enervation which I feel sometimes while listening to the inept remarks addressed to me, in the form of compliments and which I am compelled to accept with a smile, which is almost a bite. I want to shout out to the speaker: "But, my poor fellow, you ought not to speak about this subject, for you know nothing whatever about it. You do not understand the first word of it all, and you can hardly believe how little your eulogies please me, under the circumstances."

But if I answered in this way, no one would think of honoring my sincerity, or my desire to spread sane ideas, rather all would declare that I was a rude fellow, pretentious and a swaggerer, or something worse.

This is the reason that I listen, remain dumb and let the enervation gnaw at me. Some tell me: "It is better to leave to hunting that mysterious atmosphere which serves as an aureole to the Ace. If the layman were to become competent to judge, he would possibly no longer hold the same admiration for the hunters." You will admit that this suggestion is not very flattering to us. In fine, according to this suggestion, we are interesting to them only because they know nothing about our work.

All the less have we any reason to conceal the intricacies of aerial combat and it is the duty of those who use them to explain them in such a way as to render a real service to the young and to demonstrate to the greater public that if we are sometimes worth something, it is not always for the reasons which they suppose.

They say of me: "Guynemer is a lucky dog."

Certainly, I am really a lucky dog, for I have added up forty nine (this was written before the grand total was made) victories and am still alive, and I might have been killed during my first fight. If we talk this way, every person alive today is lucky; for he might have died yesterday. De la Palisse reasons in this fashion because he knows nothing about hunting by aeroplane.

But I might astonish some persons considerably if I answered: "It's a good thing that I was a lucky dog, for I have been brought down by the enemy on seven different occasions."

I know that they will rejoin that this was really luck, for I managed to escape death. But we could continue the discussion eternally on the same subject and I prefer to abstain from it. Was it luck that day, when carried along by the great speed of my Nieuport, I rushed right past a Boche, giving him a chance to puncture an arm and wound me in the jaw? Was that luck, my fall of 3,000 meters after a shell had passed through a wing of the machine? And how many episodes there are of a similar character! Certainly, I do not wish to pretend that the question of chance, which I call Providence, does not intervene in war. But between that and the assurance that every act is guided by a manifestation of a good star, there is a world of difference. The lucky dog is he, who after having done his duty throughout the war, comes back safe and sound. He is the pilot who escapes all perils, the common French soldier who has safely taken part in every offensive. But how many will they be, the actors in the tragedy who will be present when the curtain is rung down for the last time?

And if I dispute this opinion so sharply, as far as it concerns me, it is not, certes, because I am annoyed, but, on the contrary, because I believe that it is rendering a poor service to say that we succeed in any human activity through luck. Not with standing everything, we shall end by assuming a confidence which becomes exaggerated rashness under the pretext that we are a "lucky dog." Your pupils will attempt foolish imprudence's, saying "I, too, am lucky." And in space it is, nine chances out of ten, that you will think you see luck when you meet with death. It is an error of vision!

Yet if we will only eliminate this factor we shall recognize the fact that neither that unfortunate Dorme nor I are instances of the effect of chance upon the career of aeroplane hunters. He was surnamed "Invulnerable" because he almost always came back from his cruises without a scratch. We were almost astounded if his aeroplane bore the mark of a single bullet. With me, on the contrary, I had the special faculty of coming back with missiles all over my machine.

Why was there this difference? We had almost the same methods of attack. We proceeded along uniform principles, approaching the enemy to point blank distance. What then? The reason is plain: Dorme was better at maneuvering than I. He called upon his skill to help him at the moment of attack, and when he judged that he was not sure of success, he went into a spin and broke away from the duel. I, on the contrary, used the normal method of flying, never having recourse to acrobatics, unless it was the last means to be employed. I stayed close to my adversary, as if I were mad. When I held him, I would not let him go. These two systems have their advantages and their defects, which should not astonish you, for perfection is not of this world. It would be most interesting to dissect both methods, but you must see that this is impossible for me to do.

I can draw but one conclusion from these two methods of fighting, and it is of capital importance.

It is that hunting must be done according to the temperament and character of each individual hunter. If it show itself as individual prowess, all the better. This must be cried out aloud, for many young men come to the squadron with false ideas and arrested wills, planning to bring down Boches in the style of Dorme or Heurtaux.

He who has in him the quality of a champion is the pilot who has recourse to his own initiative, to his own judgment, to his own personal equation.

Georges Marie Ludovic Guynemer was born in Paris, December 24, 1894. His father, Paul Guynemer, was a retired officer, who devoted much of his time to historical research and was especially interested in tracing the Guynemer family tree back as far as the 11th century.

Georges attended a school in Compiegne and later, when twelve years of age, entered Stanislas College in Paris. At the end of the first year he was given first prize for Latin and Mathematics. In school sports he proved himself agile and ambitious, even though he was very slender and more or less delicate. He afterwards entered the School of Polytechnics and specialized in mathematics. He had been especially fond of mechanical toys and devices, building toy aeroplanes and he delighted in the study of physics and chemistry, almost blowing himself to bits on more than one occasion, with some of his chemical compounds.

At the age of twenty, Guynemer volunteered for service on November 23, 1914. On account of his physical weakness he was refused admission no less than five times, but finally succeeded in being accepted as a student mechanic, April 26th, 1915.

CHAPTER I
The First Flights

I knew the future Ace by name for several months. But I exaggerate, for they did not always pronounce his name the same: sometimes it was Guynemer, at others Guymener.

I knew from his comrades that this young man, this youth called for admiration from all who came near him or saw his work. Writing a series on "The Stirring Flights of the War" at that time, I had but one desire, to know this pilot of whom every one already spoke only with respect. He had known how to impress himself upon all by his mastery and boldness.

Thanks to some common friends, I was introduced to him one day when he came to get some apparatus at the "General Aviation Reserve." In order to converse we went to a small cafe of Bourget. I must admit that then as now it was forbidden to the military to take alcohol, so our first interview took place back of the shop, with a small glass of Cinchona cordial: the violation, you see, was quite innocuous!

There were several present. Sergeant Guynemer talked very little before so many. He made vague statements, telling of his fights piecemeal. I was interested but far from satisfied. By trade I required more precision. But my talker seems indisposed to speak before so many.

"I want to write an article about you," I said to him.

He looked at me with those piercing eyes of his, as if he were taking counsel with himself, and after several seconds, said:

"All right, but on condition that you do not mention my name!"

Such was his modesty. He would not let me publish a name which soon thereafter was to be pronounced with veneration by the entire world.

"With that understanding let us get close together at another table, where we shall be perfectly at ease as we converse."

He consented, and seemed to be relieved at not having to talk so publicly. Difficult as he had seemed to interview before, and slow of speech, when we were smoking in each other's faces, he went into all details, told me stories, not omitting a single fact by which we could follow completely his earlier combats. And every time I saw him afterwards, I found him thus: rather silent and even taciturn before a gallery, but a brilliant, precise talker when alone with me.

As soon as he began to talk aviation, and especially pursuit, he did not stop and I was always charmed with his conversation. He was inexhaustible, passing from one subject to the other, citing a fight of one of his comrades, admiring the courage of another, protesting with conviction and anger against the lack of knowledge of others, returning to the subject of conversation and then taking up another. With inexhaustible energy he seemed to be afraid that he would not have time enough to tell me all that he wanted to tell. He advised me to write an article upon a certain subject, suggested an idea to begin with, begged me to urge a reform and finally consented to take up again the purpose of our conversation, which interested me most: his victories. When I left him, I had a notebook almost filled, one pencil worn down and . . . a cramped hand. But what a harvest!

CHAPTER II
The Ace Of Aces In Action

Our first interview dates from December, 1915. Guynemer had just come from his fourteenth fight. I transcribe here faithfully the notes which I took that very day at his dictation:

"My first meeting with a Boche took place on July 19th. I was on a two seated 'Parasol' with Guerder, my mechanic, as passenger. I had promised myself for some time to undertake a pursuit in my aeroplane, but I had always been ordered on reconnaissance, photographic missions and that kind of work did not suit me at all. It is not that it is lacking in interest, but it is less stirring. It is useful, of course, but how monotonous. And, besides, it is always set aside for the newcomers in the squadrons and I wanted to show that grit was not the exclusive possession of the older men.

"A Boche had been sighted at Coeuvres and so I took flight with Guerder and was soon in pursuit of the enemy. Shortly afterwards we saw him just over Pierrefonds, but he saw us at the same moment and fled precipitately. As his plane was faster than ours there was no possibility of catching him. Nevertheless, the joy of finding our first adversary made us attempt the most impossible things. From a great distance, a very great distance, we fired at him, possibly without any real hope of hitting him, but steadily nevertheless. We pursued him as far as the

Coucy aerodrome, where we saw him alight. He must have been well satisfied with his performance: as a 'fleer' he was most remarkable. But this displeased us greatly. We had gone out to beat down a Boche (and when we left we had no doubt of success), but we had to go back empty handed.

"There we were, with these sad thoughts, when suddenly another black point appeared on the horizon. Oh, joy, hurry with all speed towards him. As we came nearer the point became larger and was soon plain, as a Boche: it was an Aviatik sailing at about 3,200 meters. He was moving towards the French lines, thinking only of what he might find ahead, but appearing not to think for a moment that an enemy bent upon destroying him was in his wake. Poor fellow, he did not dream that on his track were two young fellows determined not to return to the squadron without performing their task, two young fellows who, in total ignorance of hunting, were convinced that all game met with was to be beaten down, and believing that to return to headquarters without a Boche would mean derision.

"And we hurried towards that plane, which really belonged to us, we thought. It was not until Soissons was reached that we came up with him, and there the combat took place. During the space of ten minutes everybody in the city watched the fantastic duel over their heads. I kept about fifteen meters from my Boche, below, back of and to the left of him, and, not withstanding all his twisting, I managed not to lose touch with him. Guerder fired 115 shots, but could not fire precisely, as his gun jammed continually. On the other hand, in the course of the fight my companion was hit by one bullet in the hand and another 'combed' his hair. He answered with his rifle, shooting well. We began to ask ourselves how this duel was going to end, but at the 115th shot fired by Guerder, I had a feeling, very sweet I will admit, at seeing the pilot fall to the bottom of his car, while the 'lookout' raised his arms to heaven in a gesture of despair and the Aviatik did a nose spin, and plunged down into the abyss in flames. He fell between the trenches. I hastened to land not far away, and I can guarantee that I never felt a greater elation than at that moment.

"At last I was able to live my dream! I, who had so long desired to join in the fighting, had managed to gain a victory. What shall I say about the reception given me by the troops on the ground: ovations, congratulations, all under the vengeful cannon of the enemy. I have beaten down other Boches since that time, but when I think over my aerial duels my recollections always fly back to that first one.

"Two days later I received a letter which gave me the highest satisfaction, for it proved to me the friendliness of the infantry. They have so often said that the infantry is jealous of the aviators that I was happy at this testimony of sympathy. It proved to me that if at times the common French soldier does not love the pilots, it applies to certain exceptions of which the 'fifth arm' is not over proud."

With charming modesty Guynemer did not wish me to make a copy of the letter of which he had spoken with such deep emotion. He explained that the one who signed it might not be pleased to see it given publicity. He added that if it were printed his comrades might think that he was trying to get unfair publicity. It was only after I had promised that I would not use it that the hero allowed me to make a copy of it for my personal collection. The Ace of Aces is no more. Those who honor his memory are no longer restrained by the discretion which he showed, hence I quote the following:

"July 20, 1915.

"Lieutenant Colonel Maillard, commanding the regiment of Infantry, to Corporal Pilot Guynemer and Mechanic Guerder, of Squadron M. S. 3, at Vauciennes. The Lieutenant Colonel, the Officers, all the Regiment:

"Witnesses of the aerial combat in which you took part above their trenches, with a German Aviatik, have applauded spontaneously at your victory which terminated by the vertical fall of your adversary and they address to you their warmest felicitations and share the joy which you must have felt after so brilliant a success. *"MAILIARD"*

The official recognition followed on the next day. The Military Medal recompensed the two victors. Here is the transcript of the one to the Pilot:

"Corporal Guynemer, a Pilot full of spirit and boldness, volunteering for the most dangerous missions, after a sharp pursuit, has met a German aeroplane in a combat, which ended by setting it on fire and bringing it to earth."

Guynemer, not forgetting his friends, added to his report:

"Vedrines, who up to this time had shown me a fine spirit of fellowship, was one of the first to congratulate me. He had come up in an automobile, and seeing me so happy, so overjoyed, did not wish me to go back piloting the aeroplane: as he was afraid that I might refuse or feel hurt in some way, he explained his purpose with such fine delicacy that I could not refuse. He said that as he had been, as it were, my mentor in the squadron up to this day, he was very anxious to escort the victor of the day to the aerodrome. It was impossible for me to reject so friendly a suggestion, so it was as Vedrines' passenger that I went back to the station of M. S. 3 on the plane which had just brought me my success."

CHAPTER III
Special Missions

Eager for all the facts, I persuaded Guynemer to consult his notebook of flight, so that there be no mistake of memory, and not to omit one interesting story. He submitted gracefully to this journalistic exigency.

"It is true," said he, "I was about to forget to tell you that I had performed two special missions on September 29th and October 1st."

The special mission at that time was all the fashion. The fashion is only a mode of speech, for we never find many amateurs. It is an ungrateful task, dangerous, with many terrible results, and is executed only by volunteers. Vedrines was the great Ace: he executed seven of these. Guynemer, belonging to the same squadron, did not hesitate an instant. He offered at once to serve.

What is a "Special Mission"? The enemy having published the story of two men who have performed these missions, we are telling him nothing when we say that it has to do with two aviators departing together, going over the territory of the enemy and returning separately.

"The first," said Guynemer, "was hard enough, for the weather was execrable. I had the wind at my back on the way out, but when coming back it blew straight against me, and I was afraid I would never get back. It took three hours to complete my task, and I thought all the time that I would never be able to regain our lines.

"The second was even more fertile in incidents, and after it I swore never to try anything like it again. They had told me the place which I was to study. I left and everything went without incident, until I reached the place pointed out to me. I stopped my motor so as not to attract any notice and descended in spirals. Two fields were beneath my wings: one magnificent, a real billiard table, seeming to make despairing appeals to me; the other filled with ruts, rough, all cut up into furrows, the very last place that any one would think of landing. I did not hesitate, selecting the former. And I continued to descend. While planning downward I could not help reflecting. That green earth which seemed to have put on festal garments to receive me, was it not too beautiful to be hospitable? Attention! I looked carefully and what did I see? Steel wires all across it in treacherous fashion. It was a ruse of the Boches, a trap for pilots!

"What chance had I to be distrustful? Quickly I turned on the gas and climbed upwards, and all the more did I decide to land on the other ground, the bad place which I had just disparaged a moment before. Now it seemed most favorable. So it was, and notwithstanding several disquieting bumps on landing I had the satisfaction of finding that not a bit of my plane was damaged. Some seconds later I rose

The first flight of the Ace of Aces.

without trouble and began my flight anew. All ended well, but I had come near being singed. Really, the special mission is a mean job."

A second citation recompensed the Pilot:

"He has proved his valor, energy and coolness by accomplishing as a volunteer an important and difficult mission during stormy weather."

And we came back to hunting expeditions, for I did not dare question Guynemer about his start. I kept this subject for another time. I was afraid at this first interview of boring him with too many questions, and so I kept the recital of all his fights for another day.

CHAPTER IV
Battles In The Air

"On September 30th, when I was in a single seated plane at 3,200 meters (it is notable that all my duels in the air took place at this altitude), more than 30 kilometers within the lines of the enemy, I was challenged by a Fokker. My machine gun jammed and I could not get it working. I was in a position where I could not reply to fire. The enemy, when 50 meters from me, fired no less than 200 times, and by a miracle did no more than puncture one of my tires. But the situation might change from one moment to another, and the chance was that the Boche would finally hit me in a less kindly way. I had to find some speedy solution. A sea of clouds floated some 500 meters beneath us, and I did not hesitate, notwithstanding the advice always given us, to avoid clouds and mist, to plunge at full speed into the expanse of cloud and disappear from the eyes of my adversary, who certainly had already counted me as beaten down, to be added to the list of his conquests.

"This disappearance, which was much like the dropping of the traitor through a trapdoor in a melodrama, must have upset all the calculations of the Boche. For ten minutes I lay hidden in that sea of mist. I could see nothing and that was the main point, I was not seen. The Fokker had to stand on guard and I had to avoid falling foul of him. Here again luck helped me: I shot up, climbing rapidly. When I reached the open air, I found myself leaning on one wing, but soon regained my equilibrium. The enemy was no longer there, and I did not wait for him: I hastened to regain our lines, breathing more than one sigh of relief.

"On November 6th there was a new incident for my eighth fight and this, too, on account of my gun jamming. Really, my machine guns gave me endless trouble. I must admit that it is because I had not studied how they worked with sufficient care. But I did finally learn how to handle them, and now when they jam it is because they cannot help it. On this day my gun was frozen and refused to go off. If I had known then what I know now, I would only have had to press on the percussion cap and the frozen oil would not have resisted any longer. But the hunter has to learn how to hunt.

"I was over Rozieres-en-Santerre, at 3,200 meters, as usual, when I saw a superb 150 horsepower L. V. G. with a Parabellum machine gun.

"I began by trying to face him so as to fire, when I found that my machine gun had not the least murderous intention. It seemed as if the good Boche god were protecting him. But I, my French God, the true God, was He about to abandon me? What was I to do? No clouds about today, I must find some other way out.

"Only one resource was left, to use the enemy as a shield! I turned on one wing, passed below him and remained about two meters below the body of his machine. I regulated my speed by his, and from a distance we must have looked like one gigantic apparatus. You may be sure that I lost not a single detail of the German device. But what was the use, for I had not even a revolver to shoot with, but the Boche would have been at my mercy with the most in offensive weapon.

"He, who had me at the moment I turned, had no more warlike ardor. He must have been very much annoyed, for he had followed each move, and knew that I was very close to him, just underneath. He, too, must have had his regrets; if there had only been a trapdoor under his seat he could almost have knocked me down by a kick on the head. But, is it not true that the plane builders could not think of everything, and would hardly have dreamed that aeroplanes ever would be used for a dual parade like this. The person above hardly dared to make a motion downward for fear of coming too close to me, and being dragged down by my fall. He certainly flew perfectly straight and level. As for myself, finding it too foolish to be in this position without being able to take advantage of it, I fussed with my gun again, trying to get it to work. I had, of course, to drop the steering control. It was certainly not the moment to do such a thing. Suddenly I saw that I was about to collide with the only Boche with whom I seemed to have an understanding. Judging that the danger was imminent, I quickly gave a blow at the foot lever to the right to avoid telescoping, and in the resulting turn my left wing caught the right wing of the enemy: it was a moment of high tension, you will easily understand. But it was nothing, only a little bit of cloth was torn from my apparatus. We parted, on even wing, but re-established our relative position as if we had always sailed together in twin fashion. And I can assure you that the Boche did not try to profit by the situation: he speeded away as fast as possible, without stopping to see whether I could find my way alone. I think that if he has not yet been killed he will not soon forget this experience. The 'Siamese Twins of the Air' might well serve as the title of our joint recollections.

"But these different contests did not increase the number of my victories, so I did not find them at all to my taste."

CHAPTER V
A Battle Royal

"The 5th, 8th and 14th of December were to be more favorable for me. On the first day, while I was cruising around, I fought with an Aviatik over the forest of Ourseamp. I had been watching him for an hour and a half. He had made several attempts to cross the French lines and every time he saw me he fled, only to come back again a little later. I could not continue this game of hide-and-seek indefinitely. I dashed towards him and got him. He received me with two shots from his machine gun. I replied by a row of 47 cartridges, and almost at once saw with joy that he was falling, all awhirl. During the fall, at 200 meters below me, I beheld a really tragic spectacle: in a sudden twist of the aeroplane left to itself, one of its two passengers was thrown overboard and dashed to the earth.

"My victory was more conclusive on December 8th. I was on my way to cruise in the sector of Roye-Nesle. I had about finished, after gaining some interesting information, but not having seen a single Boche in the air. I turned towards our quarters and was getting ready to come down, when upon turning my head to see whether I had left the air clear, I saw far over the enemy lines and much higher than I was, a large, superb foe. Ah, there was the wished for prey! Without stopping to see whether I had plenty of gas aboard, I hastened towards him. He was coming towards our territory. I let him come on, for my success of the 5th, when I could find only the body of the 'Lookout,' had determined me to bring down the Boches within our lines whenever I could, if the occasion permitted. I restrained myself all I could while awaiting the arrival of my foe. It required no less than thirty minutes and I admit that I was most impatient all that time. I mapped out my plan of combat. I recalled all the conditions under which earlier fights had taken place, and drew certain conclusions, not, however, without saying to myself that my entire plan would probably not correspond with the facts. And I really preferred to have it so, that I might gain by experience a knowledge of the principles of aerial hunting.

"Finally my Boche came near. He passed over the trenches of Beuvraigne, zigzagging all the way, to see whether he was pursued, or if there was anything to fear. He was a careful man! But, nevertheless, he did not see me. I took advantage of this! I came up from the rear and overtook him in a few minutes, swooping down upon him some twenty meters below me. I fired a volley of 47 cartridges. The Boche, a large L. V. G., turned over at once and caught fire. I had hardly the time to see him pirouette in space, the effect was so sudden.

"As had been the case three days earlier, the passenger was tossed out of the apparatus by this sudden twist caused by my shots. He fell in a wood and the aviator continued his fall into the abyss!

Fire had broken out almost at once. At 1,500 meters I saw an awful thing: the pilot in his turn was tossed out of the cockpit. He had sat there motionless, jolted, tossed about like a puppet. He was dead! But his fall had been brought about by the fire. His belt being burned through, he had swayed with the aeroplane at every turn, until it turned completely over and he fell out. This sight was really tragic. The unfortunate man was dashed to bits at Tilloloy, some four kilometers from the body of his comrade. As to the aeroplane, it fell some hundred meters the other side of the line. It was really a collection of scattered elements.

"Now comes an incident which is rather amusing, proving how well I had cooperated with the other 'Arms' that day. The Boches came out of their trenches to recover the debris of the aeroplane which had made a great explosion with its bombs when it struck the ground. At the instant our artillery fired, getting several victims. The survivors did not seem any more interested in aviation and hastened to take refuge in a small neighboring house. The cannons continued and demolished the shelter, which buried in its ruins all the enemies who had deemed themselves safe there.

"Thanks to my victory, the French had accomplished a double stroke. And I was quite proud of it, I am free to admit, without any false modesty. As to my good luck, just think! At the moment I landed I did not have more than two liters of gasoline. It was high time!

"In the following week, the 14th, Bucquel and I had gone out as an escort of some bombarding planes, which were to operate upon the aerodrome of Hervilly. I sighted a Fokker, which, in the course of a fight with a Voisin, had had its observer killed: the French pilot had seen him crumple up at the stern. Bucquet started out in pursuit of this Boche, already heavily handicapped, cut off his retreat and saw but one person on board. At last I came up. The Fokker gave the impression of being abandoned, out of order. It came towards me, so to speak, as if it recognized a friend. He did not know what he was doing. Of course I took advantage of the situation; I fired 35 shots at short range, and as he was above me and my four comrades helped the enemy to go down to the nether regions, he nearly caught me as he fell.

"Soon thereafter I attacked a second Fokker (single-seat), firing through the propeller, looking much like a 14 meter Morane-Saulnier. He seemed to have a 100 horse power, single valve motor. Then came a real phantasia. We turned about one another almost vertically, less than ten meters apart, each one hoping to get the favorable position. As soon as we found the other in the line of fire we fired. I was embarrassed, for my spring was twisted and I had to work my machine gun with my hand over my head.

And in this series of meeting manoeuvers two hands were not too much.

It looked as if the fight would end in a collision. I had fired 21 cartridges when it seemed to me that the fatal telescoping was certain. I pulled on my levers and literally jumped over my adversary as a horse jumps a barrier at Auteuil. I can state that my wheels passed not more than 50 centimeters over the Bache's head. Disheartened, he preferred not to insist. I asked nothing better, for my plane was more or less injured: a valve rocker torn out, an inlet pipe mashed, the coil pierced, not counting many holes in the wings, the rudder, the body and huge notches in the propeller which had been hit by a bullet and the debris of the rocker. It had held together miraculously, notwithstanding all these breaks, and was not smashed. A descending cable was also severed. For my fourteenth fight I had been royally served."

Such was my first conversation with Sergeant Guynemer, who a few days later, December 24, 1915, in celebration of his twenty first birthday, received the Cross of a Chevalier of the Legion of Honor with this inscription:

"Pilot of Great Valor, filled with devotion and courage. Within six months he has carried out two special missions requiring the finest spirit of sacrifice and taken part in 13 combats in the air, of which two ended in the burning and downfall of enemy aeroplanes."

(Note. — Guynemer actually took part in 14, not 13 air-battles.)

Moreover, he was recompensed with a third citation:

"He has not ceased giving the finest instances of boldness, courage and self-possession in carrying out the most perilous missions successfully. He has just succeeded for the second time, on December 8th, in beating down an enemy aeroplane, its two passengers being killed."

The victory of December 5th was quite similar. Thus we have reached the fourth in the table of glory established by him, as follows :

First Boche, July 19, 1915
Second Boche, December 5, 1915.
Third Boche, December 8, 1915.
Fourth Boche, December 14, 1915.

As to "Palms," they are shown by the Military Medal, the Legion of Honor with four palms, the fruits of seven months' work.

CHAPTER VI
The Beginnings

I saw the hero a few weeks later. He had read the articles devoted to him, which I had written for various papers and magazines and thanked me not for having talked about him, but for not having made him play a "ridiculous" part.

"It is so easy," said he, "to make those persons whom we are discussing odious, even with the best intentions in the world. I was afraid that you would praise me in such a way that the reader would be disgusted. What you have written in the Journal and J'ai Vu has pleased me because of its exactness. But how the devil you understood me so fully just from my talk about my first fights is remarkable."

I explained how I had taken notes, adding: "You see, it is better to answer the questions which I put to you. In this way at least I shall make no mistakes, and I am sure that nothing will be omitted."

"You're a devil of a fellow!" And every time he met me afterwards he used the same expression, with his charming smile:

"Here is that devilish man to whom you must always tell everything."

That day I took advantage of the opening to ask him some details about his beginnings with the squadron. With his usual good grace he told me:

"You wrote, by some miracle, that I had taken up aviation after having been rejected five times. But here I must correct you. You said that I had been cured, but that is only being postponed. Let it go at that! I began by becoming a student mechanic in the school at Pau. I worked and learned all that I could with but one purpose: to become an aviation pupil. It took a long time, was very trying and discouraging! At last I gained my entrance, January 26, 1915.

"On the very next day I began training. But that is really only a way of speaking, for the training in the first few days is nothing more than shoveling snow. I put all my heart into it while waiting for better things, for I knew that the rest was fated to come in normal fashion. I had only to be patient.

"On February 1st my apprenticeship as a pilot took on aerial character. I drove a taxi and then the following week I mounted an aeroplane, going in straight lines, turning and gliding and on March 10th I made two flights lasting twenty minutes in daylight. At last I had my wings. I passed the examination next day.

Then I flew on a Bleriot, but they authorized me to try a Morane and I was sent to the school of Avord. On April 26th I received my military commission. I ought to state that during my training

I came near being scratched from the list, a certain head pilot claiming that I was foolishly imprudent because I made too difficult flights, according to his way of thinking, and because I flew when the weather was unfavorable.

He did not understand, poor man, that it was not my desire to 'play to the gallery,' but that I was working along what seemed to me reasonable lines: was not this apprenticeship to make real pilots of us? When the test was passed these pilots were to go to the front. And if they did not know all the secrets of flight, all the mysteries of aviation, they would be poor aviators and could not render the service required of them. It seemed to me that the sanest logic required that those who formed the squadron should be absolutely fit, and that for them flying should have become so automatic that they could fly in any weather and under any conditions whatever. But this was not the opinion of our head pilot. It is true that he had enjoyed no opportunity to engage in actual warfare."

It was a biting phrase and required a commentary. Guynemer was a sincere friend and a devoted comrade, but he had striking ideas and always most spirited in connection with those whom he thought lying in ambush or tricksters. These were objects of hatred to him! He hated no others. I shall take occasion to discuss his opinions on this subject. This great Frenchman could not consider those who did not perform their duty loyally and never omitted an opportunity of advising me to write an article about them. But to return to our conversation. Guynemer is now ready to take his place in the squadron.

Photograph made by Guynemer himself while he was on a reconnaisance over the German lines, showing bombs bursting around his plane.

"On May 22, 1915, 1 was ordered to leave for the General Reserve, where I received an appointment.

On June 8th I reached M. S. 3, established at Vauciennes. It was commanded by our master in all things, one of the creators of 'hunting', Captain Brocard. I found Vedrines there and he received me in friendly fashion. Famous for his special missions which added a new page to the glorious sum of his successes, he gave me all the information possible. To him I was a boy, who amused him. He took pleasure in giving me all the advice that I wanted. And there was much of this! He took me to the lines, had me visit the sector and accepted me even as a partner in a special mission, my first.

"I began my work with reconnoissances. Now this kind of work does not interest me anymore, but when we are new, and want to do something, it is really thrilling to be way up there, studying the ground, asking oneself questions with the help of the map, and above all admiring the stoicism of our soldiers who live there in those holes, beneath those murderous mounds, having as their companions the cannon, cooking pots and grenades. Poor fellows, how the aviator should love and venerate them and help them when he can! Captain Brocard is the one who has instilled into us this love for the infantry. He never misses an opportunity of making us feel the difference between them and ourselves, and really we ought to insist upon this point in all the squadrons. Much of the coldness, many of the enmities would disappear! Oh, yes, making these reconnoissances is a work which in the long run becomes fatiguing and monotonous, but what recollections are left by those first flights over the battlefield, what a splendid spectacle, and how sad!

"In order to make a reconnaissance a man must put his whole heart into it. The command wants facts, and it is indispensable to bring them to the commander as complete as possible. It is at the risk and under many perils of the pilot and I admit that I have returned frequently after more or less serious attacks. On June 17th, notably, I came back with eight wounds, another time with nine, while a tenth bullet passed only a few inches from my face. The Boche cannon shoot straight, but we have to show them that they do not frighten us."

What Guynemer did not tell me, but I learned from his comrades, was the story of one of these reconnoissances.

The last comer to the squadron, with the air of a "young girl" as Vedrines used to say, he felt in the beginning that they did not take him seriously, notwithstanding all the work that he did. He thought that they had a kind of protective friendship for him, which was pleasant, but that they had no great confidence in him. Therefore, he decided to show them something very decisive, after which they could be no longer in doubt.

One day while on a photographing mission, he was picked out especially by the aerial batteries of the enemy. According to the captain who accompanied him as a passenger, more than a thousand shells were fired at them. Without flinching from this terrific deluge Guynemer did not make a single turn to escape the attacks. He went straight towards his objective.

The reconnaissance lasted an hour. When he had finished his work the observer gave him the signal to return. But the pilot drove directly towards the guns which were trying to beat him down and holding his personal photographic apparatus out to his companion asked him to take some pictures of the mortar attacking the aeroplane.

From that day on not a person in the squadron doubted the future of this youth!

"What I must tell you," said Guynemer, modest to excess, "is the courage of the observers. When we stop to think that those officers deliver up their lives to a pilot who may make one mistake, be the victim of a moment of dizziness, or of a fainting fit, or even of a mortal wound, or anything else and that they busy themselves only with the ground and their map, in order to bring back the best possible report, we cannot admire them too much. I admit that I would not like their profession. I am not afraid, but I accept that danger against which I can fight, while the observer has to have blind confidence in his pilot and never stop to consider the steering of the aeroplane. Almost always he knows nothing whatever about the mysteries of aviating and yet he is there with you to whom he has given his life in charge. It is an art in itself and you must take into consideration these unknown artisans of victory, the most useful collaborators of the commander. I assure you that an observer like Lieutenant Colomb, for instance, has deserved well of the country."

CHAPTER VII
From Success To Success

When Guynemer became a specialist in pursuit he naturally stopped all reconnoissances and found himself assigned to a single seated aeroplane. In January, 1916, he did not add a single victory to his list, but February was to give him new success.

In April, when he came out of the hospital, I had a chance to pass a few minutes with him and Second Lieutenant Raty, one of his intimate friends, a remarkable "hunter," made a prisoner, but in whom all saw a future Ace.

Of course both of us asked the Ace, Raty, to get information about hunting and the way to fight, I to add to my documents about him whom we all considered a phenomenon, for it must not be forgotten that at that time aerial encounters were not yet so common. Indeed, on February 3, 1916, in the course of a single flight, Guynemer succeeded in getting his first official "double."

"I was making my usual round in the Roy sector," said he, "just before luncheon. I was about ending the flight, when looking around to see if I might leave safely, I saw an aeroplane in the distance. Ah! the game was coming to me. Good, all I had to do was not to let it escape. It was an L. V. G. I gave chase and soon caught up with it. He did not seem to wish to avoid the fight, as so often happens. Possibly he had not seen me after all. Being faster than he I got in back of him, opening fire at 100 meters, and firing at intervals soon exhausted the 47 cartridges of my Lewis. At that instant a cloud of smoke, which increased rapidly, made a sinister tail to the Boche, which dived, severely wounded. Alas! he fell within his own lines and I could not follow him to earth. I certainly considered that I had one enemy less, but my total was not improved and I admit that I regretted it, for I needed my fifth.

"Providence was on the watch I was coming back, thinking over the methods of fighting, considering how I had attacked, asking myself whether I would not have done better to approach from some other direction, when at almost 11:30 I found another hunting L. V. G., disguised, armed with a Parabellum. Yes, I had made a mistake just now, when I opened fire from so far away, I should have waited. At 100 meters we cannot be sure of the aim. My method, which up to this time always consisted in attacking almost point-blank, seemed to me much better. It is more risky, but everything lies in maneuvering so as to remain in the dead angle of fire. Certainly it is rather difficult, but nevertheless it can be mastered with skill.

"While going over these things to myself I had come near enough to the Boche without running any great danger. At 20 meters I fired. Almost at once my adversary tumbled in a tailspin. I dived after him, continuing to fire my weapon. I plainly saw him fall in his lines, where he was crushed. That was all right, no doubt about him. I had my fifth! I was really in luck, for less than ten minutes later another L. V. G., sharing the same lot, spun downward with the same grace, taking fire as he fell through the clouds.

"The second day afterwards, before Frise, in a new tete-a-tete with an L. V. G., I leaped forward, caught up with him, got in back of him, a little below to avoid his fire, and at 15 meters fired 45 cartridges. He swayed sadly, in the shock of death, which I was beginning to be able to diagnose, then fell like a stone, taking fire on the way. He must have been burned up between Assevillers and Herbecourt.

"Although he was really my seventh Boche, he alone gained me the honor of a special communication."

A fifth citation recompensed the Ace:

"A hunting pilot with audacity and energy for any emprise. On February 3rd he has caused the fall of three enemy aero- planes in succession, in their lines. On February 5th he attacked an L. V. G. aeroplane and beat it down in flames over the German lines."

Raty was not satisfied with mere side anecdotes; he wanted the facts as to the method of fighting. Guynemer acceded with enthusiasm:

"The most difficult thing is to compel the Boche to accept the duel. He does not lack courage, but he prefers not to run the risk of being brought down. Every time that you come up with him and that he cannot do otherwise, he conducts himself with great valor. Up to this time I have never met a cowardly opponent who inspires you with repulsion. Some defend themselves more or less expertly, others attack without method, some are especially adroit. It has seldom happened to me to return without some wounds. On several occasions my garments were drilled with holes. I took the chance that they would hit some mortal spot. On March 6th, for instance, I was in a two-seater and the union suits of my observer and myself were almost like sieves.

"Once the Boche has been compelled to accept the meeting, it is well to be on your guard, for his arms are most redoubtable. The first tactics require that you should not face the sun, lest you be dazzled. Then do not place yourself in front of the enemy, as you would offer too easy a target. The best position is at the rear, a little below, so as to render him helpless without an opportunity of returning your fire. When you have succeeded in getting in this position do not lose hold on him. You must not lose sight of one of the movements of the adversary, following him, as if moved by the same power; in a word, cling to him like a leech. And as soon as you have the Boche in the line of fire, shoot in jerks, so as not to waste shots and to fire only with good aim.

Guynemer shot down from a height of over 9,000 feet by a rench cannon—but he only suffered a bruised knee!

One of Guynemer's victims, first shot to pieces, then burned almost to a cinder.

It must not be forgotten that the belt of our Lewis guns have only 47 cartridges, while those of their Parabellum have 250. That is quite a difference.

"I set upon my rival, but this is a method which has its drawbacks. We never know when he will regain his hold and 'dress' you in turn. Surprise is the best way to conquer and the sudden attack is one that has always served me well. When I prolong the attack, it is because I had no luck, but it is stronger than I; when I have a Boche in front of me, I cannot make up my mind to let him go. I know them too well: they will say when they go back that they have beaten me down."

CHAPTER VIII
A Game With The Boche

"One victory which amused me greatly was that which I carried off on March 12th. I was a hundred leagues away from where they awaited me.

"I was then ordered to go and re-enforce the aviation of the Verdun army, which had great work to do against the fifth Boche arm, really redoubtable in this sector. Here
we encountered all kinds of new models of hunting aeroplanes. We were therefore certain to have plenty to do. Before Navarre's arrival the supremacy of the air plainly belonged to the enemy, all during the month preceding the offensive of February 21st. Navarre accomplished many deeds of prowess, and equalized the chances of the belligerents. Now we had to gain the advantage over them. Thus several squadrons, including No, 3, had been appointed.

"We left on the 12th. I had my machine gun ready for anything that might occur, but I did not think that during the trip I would have any opportunity to use it. There I made a mistake: near Thiescourt I caught sight of a two-seated L. V. G. I overtook it near Ribecourt. A few shots, fire! It was all over: one less Boche, one more for me. I thought that this success out of the beaten track, I might say, was to bring me some stunning work when I was on the track.

"So on the next day, it was the 13th, but an aviator cannot stop on account of superstitions. I left with the firm determination to bring down at least two, for there were so many in the sky around Verdun. I began by putting to flight what I think was a group of reconnoitering aeroplanes, a pity I could not catch up with them. On the way back I saw two Boches. There were the two that I was to bring down. I rushed at them, speeding all I could, getting below one, to the rear, a little to one side, firing seven shots at point blank distance. He turned about and went away with lead in his wings, but I could not take up time with one of his kind.

"As to the other, he was certainly an Ace. He was not afraid and fired as hard as he could. My aeroplane knows something about that. I wanted to get myself under the body of his machine to bring him down safely. Unfortunately I had speeded up too much, going faster than he, and I passed beyond him. Quickly the Boche took advantage of the situation and sent a hot fire at me. He could shoot at me as he pleased. My cape shot to bits, flew in ribbons. A deflected bullet struck me in the face, slashed my cheek and nose and two bullets went through my left arm. I still have a splinter in my jaw and the surgeons say it is better to leave it there. It is a souvenir, so long as it is a fetch and allows me to avenge myself. In fine, I was sprinkled all over.

"I bled freely and actually suffered. I had to look out that I did not 'drop like an apple.' I studied the situation hastily. I let myself fall, plunging downward 300 meters to make him think that I had been knocked down. And as now another aeroplane came up to help my rival in the attempt to finish me, I turned about and steering with one hand, I succeeded in regaining our lines, landing at Brocourt.

"I shall never be able to express my regrets at having to leave my comrades. I considered it a feast to be able to take part in the great battle. One mistake on my part, the cutting of a vein by my adversary was enough to keep me from the front.

But soon I was almost well and I tell you that I determined to 'put in some good licks' to compensate for lost time. They would have to pay me for my sojourn at the hospital."

And then came two new citations, the sixth and seventh:

"On March 6th he has engaged in a combat with a German aeroplane, in the course of which his aeroplane, his garments and those of his observer were pierced by bullets. On March 12, 1916, he attacked a two-seated German aeroplane and beat it down in flames in the French lines: 21 aerial battles in eight months; 8 German aeroplanes beaten down, 7 of these within or near the French lines."

"Second Lieutenant Guynemer: ordered to rejoin the Verdun army, beat down an enemy aeroplane on the way. Hardly arrived he took part in five aerial battles. In the course of the last, being caught between two enemy aeroplanes, he had his left arm pierced by two bullets. Hardly was he improved when he took up again his work at the front."

We must recollect that the first Boche dates from July 19, 1915. In less than eight months the Ace of Aces had seen seven palms find a place on his War Cross!

He was to progress much more rapidly at his work!

As he left us Guynemer expressed his high appreciation of the Baby Nieuport, which had, nevertheless, been the cause of his being wounded on account of its great speed. Enthusiastic about its' manageability, he claimed that this apparatus could play its part well against the best of the enemy fighting aeroplanes.

CHAPTER IX
Convalescence In The Open

Just like Nungesser who, healed twice, never wanted to leave the army and always refused furloughs for convalescence, using the time profitably to increase the slaughter of Boches, as if up there they could not dare suspect a wounded man, just like Dorme, Triboulet and Matton, Guynemer would not rest once he had left the hospital. It is by signs like these that we find the souls of great heroes who know nothing about vacations, even for their health, so long as others are fighting.

And there is no ostentation in actions like these. Matton and Triboulet found death during these furloughs which they refused. If they had listened to the surgeons they might still be among us.

Guynemer himself did not even tell Raty and me of his decision when he saw us. Was it not beautiful, that youthful action prompted by the purest filial piety? This great hero of the air had done something to please everyone and his father, may I not say, just for once. He was not strong and should have rested. His parents wanted him to do so. A too hasty return to the squadron would have been disastrous to his health. Boche hunter, he wished to continue his work of convalescence in the air. What was he to do in this conflict between feelings equally noble and to be respected?

"The Winged Sword of France."

Guynemer always found quick and fitting solutions of difficulties: yes, he would obey his family by going near them at Compiegne, but at the same time he would serve France. Not far from his paternal home, at Vauciennes, his Baby Nieuport rested in a hangar, and it was once more to carry him into those great open spaces searching for the enemy whenever the atmosphere permitted.

One of the hero's sisters was entrusted with the task of studying the atmosphere at dawn every day to see if it were "Boche weather." And as soon as it was light enough, slyly, like a boy going out to muse in the fields notwithstanding the orders of his elders, the Second Lieutenant Ace came down from his room and mounted his chariot for a glorious assault.

He was convinced that no one in the house suspected his escapades except his sister. How poorly he understood the heart of a father and mother! M. Guynemer has told me of the anxieties; the worries lived through during that convalescence. The boy had gone. Would he come back? Would some hateful enemy appear on the way and prevent his return to the bosom of his family? The minutes of anxiety were as long as centuries. Magnificent instants, but how moving! And the loving mother did not dare show her son that she was not deceived by his stratagems: she did not wish him to see her when she watched him fly away. But she wished to send after him one look of love, as a benediction that should guard him against traitorous attacks. Through the blinds she watched him depart in the service of his Country and when she saw her boy draw far away, she turned back, so often with tears in her eyes.

Here is one of the most moving pages in the hero's life. This feigned ignorance on the part of the parents, the plotting of brother and sister. Only persons with hearts can appreciate the situation and marvel.

Guynemer, face to face with his family, pretended that he would run no danger. He insisted on his own prudence. Nothing serious could happen to him, because he avoided all risks. Yes, their son spoke just this way. But as soon as he began to turn the conversation upon the subject which was all his life, the comforting words which he had spoken were at once contradicted by the many adventures and varied anecdotes which he recalled. No peril had been too great for him. He played with danger and looked for it. Thus it happened at his first fight, after having been wounded, he exposed himself to the fire of the enemy without stopping an instant to fire back. He was content to manoeuver and wait. A second baptism of fire, voluntary, terrible, admirable, which had but one purpose: to find again the mastery for the great fighter of the skies!

CHAPTER X
Guynemer Plays A New Game

It was only after several months that I saw our hero again. He had just beaten down his eighteenth official adversary and had been brought down by the cannon. I had to recall his victories to refresh his memory. His recollections were all confused; he confounded one success with another. Happily, I had the full list on a piece of paper. This made it possible for me to secure the desired information, and was well worth the compliments with which the Ace repaid me for what he called my patience.

"It was June 28th before I began to add up again. I was cruising around with Chainat when we met French reconnoitering and photographing division. We thought that in order to get any game we would have to fly above our comrades. The photographing aeroplane is always prey sought for by the enemy. We climbed up above 4,500 meters and waited. Our hopes were soon realized. Two L. V. G.'s approached and darted forward. They had not seen us. We dived; at 4,200 meters we were upon them. We selected one, and speedily had it tumbling in flames on our territory near Rosieres en Santerre. I had taken part in three fights that day. On the next day I was less fortunate and came back with several bullets in my aeroplane and two longitudinal spars of one wing broken.

"To discuss all of my combats is impossible; they were too many. Almost every day now I had one. However, I recollect that I was brought down most beautifully on July 6th and this incident is not on your list, so you see it is not absolutely complete. Does that bother you?

"On this occasion I certainly had to deal with a Boche Ace. He succeeded in damaging my propeller and cutting two of my cables. Much against my will I had to withdraw.

"Most of the aerial combats today take place between groups of five, six, seven, ten aeroplanes. The enemy has adopted hunting tactics which are dangerous. We can no longer laugh at him and say that if we rush to attack he is ready to run away. If we miss one, and he pretends to run away, the others are there to cut off your retreat. You must consider manoeuver and leave nothing to chance.

"My tenth Boche dates July 16th. Oh! he was as easy as anything. It was an L. V. G. Heurtaux and I had attacked him from the rear and had sent him down in flames, crashing to earth near Barleux. He landed on the cabane! This demi-looping seems not to have been tried by the amateurs of Kultur. On the 28th I began by attacking a group of four, one of which was brought down, certainly because I fired at him at close quarters. A few minutes later I met another squadron of four. The result was far less satisfactory. As soon as they saw me the Boches fled to right and left. Only one could be pursued, and I did not miss him, sending the 250 bullets of my Wickers through him. But at the last shot a blade of my propeller flew into the air. My motor began to revolve all ways; I was shaken as if in a basket. I could not pay any more attention to my adversary. I had to content myself with getting back as well as I could: gliding, I would land at the first aerodrome I found.

"My 'probably downed' foe was in a similar condition, for he had fallen in sight of the English trenches and the observers on the ground saw to his end.

"At last I reached my dozen on August 3rd. As on July 16th, I brought down my adversary near Barleux; I had attacked him while accompanied by Heurtaux."

"But how about your attack on the trenches with your machine gun on August 7th?"

"Ah, yes, that was a new game. Very amusing! Lieutenant Heurtaux and I had decided to try it so as to prove to the brave ground soldiers that we did not forget them and that we wished to take part in the dangers which they faced. When they attacked we asked permission to collaborate with them. Having spied out some nests of machine guns which were trying to mow down attacking ranks of assailants, we came down, almost to the ground, and began firing at these objectives, as well as upon groups of men, batteries and trenches. The poor troopers who were in the furnace thought no more of their own danger, but shouted to us in their enthusiasm. I admit that this testimony of satisfaction awarded under such circumstances made us quiver with joy."

CHAPTER XI
Citations Of Victory

"My succeeding victories were rapid, most happily, for I had to compensate for several mishaps. On August 17th I downed an Aviatik with three shots. That was my thirteenth. On the 18th I did even better: I attacked my Boche to the west of the woods of Madame, between Bouchavesnes and Clery, and at the second shot he fell to pieces. This is the best I had done: brought down two aeroplanes with five cartridges. Here is the solution of the high cost of living. We must economize! We must economize!

"On August 20th I came up with a Boche, but was not able to get him. However, I have the conviction that he will never get me.

On the next day I attacked two aeroplanes at point-blank distance. I killed one passenger, but I could not see the end because I had to turn upon the other machine. I had made a mistake, for it fled at once. On the same day I killed another passenger. All the observers of this sector will certainly want to pass as pilots. At last came a fight which was not so favorable for me, and the L. V. G. which I attacked came back at me with full force, sending a bullet through my tank, among other things. One ball touched the end of my finger, dying there, after having passed through everything else in its way. It was a great borer. I admit that it worked effectively.

I asked no more, but hastened to land in our second trenches.

"I took my revenge on September 4th: my adversary (the fifteenth) turned a complete somersault, falling near our lines. On the 9th I did for two which were not counted for me.

"As to my latest, it was on September 15th that I brought him down. He was the finest and fattest of a group of six.

"I increased my altitude: finding that my cruising around 3,000 meters was fantastic. In the spring of this year I passed to 4,000 and now I operated at 5,000 or higher. In my day's work of the 15th I had given battle six times at point blank distance. The one which ended successfully gave me an opportunity of seeing my adversary go all to bits in space. His wings buckled up and then broke away on each side, the rest, body and equipment, ran a race to the earth with them. That was my second battle that day. At the fifth I killed the passenger and would not have given much for the pilot, but the aeroplane seemed to be under control when it reached the ground."

Before having him tell me all about that glorious day, September 23rd, which came near ending most tragically for him, let us note the citations which Guynemer earned by these various victories:

8th. On June 22nd he took part in three aerial combats: in the course of one of these he beat down

*Brought down by a Bôche, but within the French lines.
The machine alone was injured.*

a German aeroplane, after his apparatus had been struck by enemy projectiles.

9th. On July 16th, 1916, he brought down his tenth enemy aeroplane, which fell in flames in the enemy lines.

10th. On July 28th, 1916, he brought down his eleventh enemy aeroplane.

11th. On August 3rd, 1916, he brought down his twelfth enemy aeroplane.

12th. On the 17th and 18th of August, 1916, he brought down two enemy aeroplanes in front of the French trenches.

13th. On the 4th and 16th of September, 1916, he brought down his fifteenth and sixteenth enemy aeroplanes.

CHAPTER XII
Struck By A Shell At 3,000 Meters

Here is what is reported of his exploits of September 23rd, described to me by the Ace of Aces on the second day thereafter:

"14th. On September 23rd, 1916, seeing a group of three enemy aeroplanes subjected to the fire of our special artillery, he gave them battle resolutely, beating down two of them and putting the other to flight. At this moment he received the full force of a shell upon his own aeroplane and only by prodigies of skill was he able to regain our lines, where he fell over, only slightly wounded."

It is impossible to give the least idea of the good humor and animation with which Guynemer gave me all the details of this series of varied feelings. I am trying to report his narrative as faithfully as possible, so as to let it retain his characteristic style as nearly as may be. The hero, who two days before had almost met his death under horrible conditions, laughed at the details of the trying adventure, and found amusing expressions to give an idea of the situation in which he found himself. No one would have thought for a moment that the shadow of death had lowered so deeply over his head.

"For the sixth time I was brought down, and that was fame indeed! And I was thinking what our poor artillerists would have done if they were told that they had just killed me! I had to ask myself again how it was that fate, for which we all wait, but for which I do not look, had not been reserved for me. It is a mystery to me.

"The day had begun well. It could not really end tragically. At the very moment when I least expected it Providence intervened, and I assure you that if I were not a believer, this celestial protection would have proved it to me, when the irreparable seemed about to happen, that there is really a Superior Power which directs our acts and makes us the poor puppets which it compels to do its will.

"On the day before I had the opportunity of bringing to the ground a Fokker, which I do not count at all, for it was too far over the enemy lines. On the next day, September 23rd, I started to make my rounds about luncheon time. I like this time especially because the Boche thinks that we are eating, enjoying our coffee, or digesting our meal and profits by these two or three hours to try incursions over our lines.

"I did not have to wait long for my luck. I soon saw one of my companions caught among some five Boches, acting along their well-known tactics, three in line above and two below. I left the Frenchman to deal with the latter and went straight at the trio. At 11:20 I sent one down in flames towards Aches. He fell so suddenly, so brutally that those below him looked at one another, thinking that it must be one of them. My comrade also even thought that he had triumphed. As for me, I continued my work. Thirty seconds after my first success I succeeded in putting out of commission, absolutely helpless, a second Fokker: the passenger had been killed, as I plainly saw, and as for the pilot, he was not much better, but I could not see him. He fell near Carrepuy.

"There was now only one in front of me, and he fearfully accepted the challenge. Poor type indeed! At 11:23, after only two shots, he went to join his comrades, blown up, pulverized, also set afire. He fell not far from our lines about 300 meters, near Roye."

A soft boiled egg for Guynemer! Just put an egg in boiling water when the Ace of Aces begins a battle, you wait until he has downed three Boches, you take out the egg and it is done to a turn. What a triumph for the restaurant menus!

If you want me to I will guarantee that these three minutes are exact by the clock. So much for the soft boiled egg which can be scooped up in a spoon.

"I had hardly finished my third, contemplating the immensity of the azure heavens from my 3,000 feet, which I had cleared so completely and looking to see if there were no other amateurs, when suddenly, thirty seconds later, a shell struck one of my wings with all its force. The left wing was torn to shreds. My aeroplane seemed mortally wounded. The canvas floated in the wind and was torn to shreds as we fell. My apparatus fell, broke apart, crumpled up in the abyss, unable to bear me any longer. I really felt the call of death and I seemed to be hastening towards it. It seemed that there was nothing to prevent my crashing to the earth. My Boches were well avenged. A tail spin, terrible, fearful, began at 3,000 meters and continued to 1,600 meters.

"I felt as if I were indeed lost, and all that I asked of Providence was that I should not fall in enemy territory. Never that! They would have been too happy. Can you think of me buried with my victims? But I was powerless to exert my will, my aeroplane refused to obey.

"At 1,600 meters I tried anyway. The wind had driven me almost over our lines. I was already half happy. Now I dreamed of being interred with sympathetic comrades following my body. That was not a fine dream, but at least it was better than the other.

"I had no longer to fear the pointed helmets. But nevertheless I felt all that death might be and it was not a pleasant thought. The fall continued. The steering gear would not respond to my tugging. Nothing worked. I tried it to the right, to the left, pulling, pushing, but got no result. The comet did not slow a bit, I was drawn invincibly towards the earth where I was about to be crushed.

"There it was! One last brutal effort, but in vain. I closed my eyes, I saw the earth and I was plunging towards it at 180 kilometers an hour, like a plummet. A terrible crashing, a great noise, I looked around: there was nothing left of my Spad.

"How did it happen that I was still alive? I asked myself, but I felt that it was so and that was enough. However, I think that it was the straps which held me in my seat which had saved me. Without them I would have been thrown forward or would have broken some bones. On the contrary, they were dug deep into my shoulders, a silent proof doubtless that I should give them full consideration. Yes, truly, had it not been for them, on thinking it over, I would certainly be dead now.

"It is infinitely funny when you recall those instants of anguish, lived through like a nightmare. All day yesterday I was utterly stupefied. A curious impression! But see, today I am feeling fine, almost ready to begin again!

"Ah! the artillerists who had hit me, what faces they made when I landed a few meters from their battery. They were terribly distressed and I had to restore their morale. They were sure they had killed me. Never the less this is a proof that our anti aerial guns are effective. To hit a Spad at 3,000 meters is precision unknown heretofore.

"After the artillerists came the infantry men to pick up the pieces. Seeing that they did not have to carry me in a litter, they wanted to take me up from the ground and carry me in triumph, not stopping to think about my knee which was giving me considerable pain. And the brave soldiers ended by marching ahead of me, singing the "Marseillaise" at the top of their voices. It was a moving sight, and I

18ème Escadron
Aviation militaire
École de Pau.

23 Décembre 1914

Soldat Guynemer, engagé volontaire
élève mécanicien à l'école d'aviation
militaire de Pau
à Monsieur le Ministre de la Guerre
12ème Direction
Cabinet du Directeur
Bordeaux

Objet:
Brevet de
pilotage.

J'ai l'honneur de vous demander
de bien vouloir m'admettre dans le
personnel naviguant comme élève pilote.
J'ai déjà exécuté des vols comme passager.

Georges Guynemer

— avis du Commandant de l'École —
Très bon jeune soldat — Extrêmement sérieux ; ...
... parfaitement à sa place comme élève pilote.
Très intelligent — ... instruction ... — À jeter ...
... fait l'instruction d'élèves pilotes
Engagé volontaire pour la guerre

*Guynemer's application to the Minister of War for a Pilot's
License, endorsed most warmly by the head of
his Aviation School.*

hardly regretted having been brought down from the sky so roughly.

"Notwithstanding my wound, I went to view the remains of my Boche whom I had brought down first. The pilot whom I had killed had on his body a card, almost burned up, on which a feminine hand had written these words: 'I hope that you will bring back many victories.' Poor fellow, after all, even if he was a Boche!

"I did not want any furlough, but my chief insisted that I rest a few days. He could not understand that I felt perfectly well after that hard knock and I leave it to you to judge. Admit that 48 hours after that bump I am not at all ill."

CHAPTER XIII
A Long Chase

Guynemer left us. He had come in search of one of his friends, Adjutant Lemaitre, to take him home to dinner, after which they were to spend a few days with his family.

In the first week in October he took his place again at the front. Four days afterwards, on the 9th, he brought down an aero plane over Villers Carbonnel, but could not have it made official. On the next day, a similar success, similar result. On the 20th he killed the passengers in two aeroplanes but could not bring the machines to earth. And on November 3rd another Boche, unofficial. It was bad luck for Guynemer, but no less for our aviation record, for the probable victories of our Ace are always certain. Very many more of our enemies were certainly brought down than he could reckon. It mattered little to him. He claimed the right to add to his list, not those whom he was certain he had destroyed, but only those where others had witnessed his exploit. He was a good sport and never argued. What did he care about one Boche more or less; he knew that when he wanted to he could add to his list at will, and Guynemer's will was written with a capital W.

An instance may prove this. After his prowess of September 23rd some jealous inefficient fellows tried to spread the rumor about him whom they envied, but whose glory they wished to dim. According to them it was enough for Guynemer to say that he had achieved a victory for it to. be made official, without any discussion. But we have just seen, on the one hand, how indifferent the Ace was about successes which he had the right to claim and on the other hand the strictness of the authorities on allowing credit to him. Guynemer certainly was a phenomenon, but he enjoyed no special favors. His chiefs had the tact not to increase his list, in Richthofen style, for his well-known uprightness and proverbial intrepidity placed him above any such procedures.

"My victories," he used to say, "are indisputable and I would not accept the credit for one of which I was in the least doubt. I wish everyone would do the same."

With all of his youthful fire and enthusiasm Guynemer pursued with hatred those whom he thought unworthy of their rewards. He would have liked us to publish their names in all the papers. As to what was said about him he always used the same words: "It's all the same to me, they may say what they please, all I have to do is bring down the Boche, that is the essential thing, and those who do not believe it may come and see."

On November 10th Guynemer began to add some more items to his record. On that very day he achieved a double stroke:

"The day before I really had some hard luck. Three times up in the air, eight fights, not one victory. I knew very well that I had been attacked by a group operating with remarkable celerity, but that was no excuse for accomplishing nothing. So the next day I decided to rip up something.

"I had gone a long way over the enemy lines when I saw four aeroplanes, two Albatroses and two Aviatiks, the hunting planes to protect the others intent upon reconnoitering. They certainly intended taking observations along our front. I was 4,000 meters up. I hid myself in the clouds, turned after them, tracking them down like Sherlock Holmes on a trail!

"For 70 kilometers I continued the pursuit! It seemed a long time to me and I was disturbed. I was afraid of being recognized, not afraid of fighting with the four adversaries, for that was what I wanted, but I was afraid of being obliged to land and being captured alive in case of any accident to my machine. I did not want to be a prisoner. Death is the risk of the profession, but far rather that than captivity. I listened very attentively to the action of my motor, as a mother listens to the breathing of her child, when it is not very well.

"I still remained in the wake of my rivals. When I saw that at last they were nearing our trenches, where they were about to commit indiscretions which I should prevent, I rushed at the group. I was 3,600 meters up.

"The first which I attacked fell in flames at the fifteenth shot, near Nesles. I then continued the pursuit and a few instants later pounced upon an Albatros: at the third shot the observer was killed, and then it was the pilot's turn. Ten shots more and the machine turned over, crumpled up and crashed down in a field within our lines, 500 meters from the road to Amiens, along the Morcourt ravine.

"It was about 2 o'clock in the afternoon, I had been flying five hours since morning. Now I could take a rest and I went to pay my respects to my victims. The aeroplane was a two seated Albatros with a 220 horsepower Mercedes motor. This motor had dug into the ground two meters deep. The pilot was lying all crushed to bits under the machine gun. In the center of his skull was a small red hole. Not a scratch on his hands. We raised him up, and his arms and legs cracked in sinister fashion, all disjointed. At a distance of 50 meters from him we found the Second Lieutenant Observer: his contracted hand held a Browning.

"I picked up the plate of the machine and took the pilot's helmet, pierced by a single bullet."

This victory earned a fifteenth palm on Guynemer's War Cross :

"Always as eager as courageous, on November 10th, 1916, he brought down his 19th and 20th German aeroplanes."

This was the third double stroke made by the Ace of Aces. Notwithstanding the fact that the days were not favorable for aviation now, he managed to add three more victories to the list during the month of November. As was his habit, he went looking for the Boche in the air at the luncheon hour, upon the principle that at this time the enemy was less on his guard.

On the 16th he beat down the twenty first victim at 1:40 P. M.; on November 22nd another doublet: at 2:45 the twenty-second fell all aflame near Saint Christ and fifteen minutes later the twenty third fell on fire in the Faloy region. At 3 :10 a third was damaged, but it was not official. Guynemer was pursued by bad luck for his second "Triple" was not made official, any more than the one of September 23rd.

Now, naturally the sixteenth citation, which, however, makes an error in the champion's count, one of the two Boches of November 22nd being made official only as a sequel:

"Fighting ever with the same fine courage against enemy aeroplanes, he brought down on November 16th and 22nd his twenty first and twenty second German planes, both falling on fire."

CHAPTER XIV
Guynemer Celebrates His Birthday With A Boche

The series continues. I did not have the pleasure of seeing Guynemer for several weeks, having to be satisfied with the news which came to me from the squadron. More over all this series of victims has, so to say, no history. Guynemer generally rose at a group, picked out the one which was most favorably situated for his purpose, fired a few shots, and had nothing more to do than to watch this Boche fall, while the others fled. On December 26th, to celebrate his twenty second birthday, he brought down his twenty fourth at 9:45, making him fall 500 meters east of Misery; the next day at 11:45 he dropped his twenty fifth near La Maisonnette.

He went to Paris for a few days to try to carry out a plan which he had cherished for a long time.

The report of his death was circulated at this time. According to well informed persons he had been the victim of a jealous husband of the Place Pigalle. They did not say when it happened. And there were some who believed these absurdities, born at regular intervals in the brains of astonished idlers because they did not see the idol of all the French people mentioned in the official announcements for a few days. So as to seem to know, they said any old thing, but they must have known the Ace very poorly to suggest such an end for him.

Guynemer proved his resurrection by an admirable series running up to the end of January: in four days he gained five victories, although the days were very short and extremely cold, and the atmospheric conditions were most unfavorable.

Before giving the account of these con- tests, here are the series of citations:

"18th. This brilliant hunting pilot, on December 26th and 27th, brought down his Twenty fifth and twenty sixth enemy aeroplanes. (The text of the seventeenth citation is lacking.)

"19th. This brilliant hunting pilot, on January 23rd and 24th, brought down his twenty seventh and twenty eighth enemy aeroplanes.

"20th. This brilliant hunting pilot, on January 25th and 26th, brought down his twenty ninth and thirtieth enemy aeroplanes."

When Guynemer came to see us he was telling the story of those three glorious days to Captain G., the eminent technician on shooting, whom the Ace held in high estimation, and to me:

"I felt in fine trim to go after a Boche and wanted to try and demonstrate that even in Winter, if we want to, we can add to the list. For there are quite a number of persons who state that Winter is not propitious for aviation and they take advantage of it by not flying. You know that phrase circulated in some places: 'Bad weather for aviation, but what

A page from Guynemer's note-book of flight, which records his first victory, July 1, 1915.

La Sixième Victoire.

fine weather for aviators!' Well, that is not true at all. If we really want to do so, we can work just as well in Winter. It is not because the days are short that we do not perform the missions ordered. It is stupidity of conception. But to prove it we must not be satisfied with talking about it, we must bring down a Boche. This is what I tried and I am happy to have succeeded, for now those who continue to assert the opposite had better admit plainly that they have collapsed.

"And really my five victories were not so difficult to win as might have been supposed. Besides, I might add that it was only an embarrassment of choice, which shows that the moment the Boches find it to be a good time to fly, we ought to have the same opinion and act upon it.

"On the 23rd I found no difficulty in beating down in 40 minutes an aeroplane near the railway station of Chaulnes, at 10:50, and another in the Maurepas region at 11:30. Everything was very easy.

"On the 24th I was at work in the morning again. I started fighting with a group of five single-seaters which were 2,400 meters high. I was much higher and came down as fast as I could to disturb their peace. I placed myself in a position in which they could not fire back at me, as nearly as I could, but I did not succeed perfectly, for they cut one of my bracing wires. We went down, firing at one another until we were about 400 meters above Roye. At the very moment when I was in a fine position to get this victim, my motor stopped.

By the time I had it going again the Boche was far away. A few instants later, a similar meeting, same stoppage, but I had had the time to fire and did not care if my motor did 'lay down' on me. I could not follow my adversary in his fall, I was so busy with my machine. He seemed to me to have lost control entirely, although I did not think that he was beaten down."

"But the prisoners of my thirtieth, of January 26th, helped to make official this victory: they told us that the Boche, falling near Etelfay at Conencourt, had struck the ground with the observer killed and the pilot so severely wounded that they had to amputate a leg. It was really luck, and I admit that I had no regrets at having left him alive, even though he was a Boche.

"To come back to January 24th. After getting my motor to work normally, or nearly so, I suddenly saw some characteristic puffs not far from me. It was our cannon which were firing at a Rumpler with two machine guns. The fight did not last long: the Boche fell within our lines at Lignieres at 11:50. The pilot had a bullet in one lung, the passenger another in one knee. But the tanks were pierced and afire, causing the loss of my adversaries.

"The second day afterwards, my aeroplane having a wheel broken on account of the frost and having been damaged in other ways, I took flight on a comrade's Spad. In action worried me and the wait for my 'taxi' seemed to be indefinitely prolonged.

"And this flight was one of the most happy of my entire career. In any case, it proves, my dear Captain," Guynemer added, addressing Captain G., "that it is better to work with your head than with the most highly perfected machine gun. It is true that I prefer to use both! But I had only the former and I had to be content with it, did I not?"

CHAPTER XV
A Battle Without A Gun

"It was noon. An enemy aeroplane soaring at 3,800 meters. I climbed, and climbed until I was above him. He commenced to attack, and I fired back. Ten shots and my weapon failed. I could do nothing to get it to work again. What was I to do? Was I simply to leave? That would have been most annoying, for he was a fine bird. Or should I go ahead? Possibly, but how? I had ammunition but nothing with which to fire it. So much the worse! A rather foolish idea ran through my brain. I was going to try to get him at a disadvantage, while avoiding his fire as much as possible, for I assure you that his gun was still in good working order.

"We came down to less than 2,000 meters. I followed him unceasingly, trying not to let him know my inferiority in weapons. I shot upward and dived down at him and he continued to descend. I put myself some ten meters behind him. His passenger could not fire at me, but he pretended to be about to shoulder me aside, when I came up on either side. Soon I began the same manoeuvers over again and he quietly allowed me to do it. How would it end? We were traveling rapidly towards the French lines, and did not stop coming closer to the ground. We were only a few meters away. No, he will never consent! It is impossible! But yes, there can be no mistake. My Boche is going to our place. He was afraid and landed in our lines. He surrendered!

"What a joy! I had won my thirteenth victory by a bluff. It was a double victory, for through him I was able to confirm my victory of the morning. There was but one shadow on the picture, he had found time to set fire to his machine before it was captured. He admitted to us that he belonged to Squadron A, 226, made up of Albatros machines.

"We had begun our aerial jousting above Mouchy and it was between Montdidier and Compiegne that my victims had alighted, not far from the villa where my parents lived.

"I admit, when I told my prisoners that I could not have done anything to hurt them and that they really had me at their mercy, the expression on their faces amused us immensely. My first shots were so effective that they were not anxious for any more. Yes, but the others could not get to them."

I have seldom seen Guynemer so happy as when he told of this fight, which, more than anything else, proved his complete mastery, his science of air work, his bravery, deliberation and implacable determination.

CHAPTER XVI
The Outrages At Nancy

The youthful pilot Rene Altmayer, who fell for France and had become noted through his articles signed "Fortunio," sent me what he called a Winged Prose Poem: "The Avenging Storks," from which I make these extracts:

"I want the reader to know, how, after clearing the skies of the Somme, Guynemer and his valiant companions purified the heavens so continuously outraged over Nancy.

"It was one calamity among many. It seemed as if fate were against the unhappy city of Lorraine.

"The black birds, ever the black birds!

"Every day we had to record the death of workmen, fallen upon a real field of honor, at the anvil or the lathe, the death of innocent women and children.

"For three years now, said an old inhabitant of Nancy, women and girls have been assassinated by German bombs; we live in a nightmare every instant.'

"Every day, over the crests of the surrounding hills, all buried in mist, the city has seen with horror the approach of the two horsemen of the Apocalypse of Saint John: War and Death, perched upon their gigantic and sinister mounts.

"This menacing apparition lasting a little while, is blotted out by a cloud, as of blood, the two scourges fleeing towards other accursed places, or to curse them.

"The light of the sun itself seems less brilliant and its rays are less warm. An inexplicable uneasiness weighs upon man and beast and all living things. The leaves of the trees rustle no more, stopped by some higher power. In the fields the birds cease their songs and hide in the thickest foliage. All is dumb. The oppression becomes more and more heavy. In the broad meadows the red and white cattle look restlessly at the
horizon and then lie down, stretching out their long necks in fear amid the damp grass.

"This strange calmness, this impressive silence are but the advance signs of the daily stormy tempest, of the cataclysm which at the Equinox in hot countries, ruins in a few instants the luxurious crops of the rich earth and transforms into debris the picturesque homes of the colonists and natives.

"Sadness fills the towns and country. The workmen continue their arduous labors, with painful apprehension in their souls. The few stragglers flee to shelter. From all sides the sweet toned bells, in their high belfries, still standing as if in supreme defiance, sending a sinister knell, painful, heavy, fateful, over the city like a voice of agony.

"It seems to say in its raucous language:

"Brave people, take care, danger threatens."

"And now very soon, on the distant horizon, over the edge of the clouds, which become dark, appear little black specks which move with strange rapidity. They approach the city, increasing quickly in size accompanied by a deep humming, filled with menace and hate.

"A sorrowful cry passes speedily, terrifyingly, over the city: 'The black birds! The black birds!'

"There they are, in great numbers, spreading their shadows over the earth from sinister wings.

"There are slow vultures, enormous, bearing death. About them cleave the rapid hawks, with pointed wings and sharp beaks ready for the fight.

"From the suburbs of the city, their nests hidden under large trees, white pigeons hasten forth to pursue the savage horde. A superb flight of courage and audacity, generous thrusts, filled with useless heroism, alas! too often. Their poor wings, ill adapted for the race, do not help them to rise with sufficient rapidity. Their beaks, formed for other work than battle, do not serve them at the required moment. Never the less, they ascend and throw themselves upon the invaders, who hastily sow death beneath them.

"In the wide spaces there are tragic struggles. The powerful ranks of vultures and hawks ferociously crunch the bodies of the poor pigeons. Their sharp beaks dig into the flesh with a terrible grating of teeth, their claws tear them apart. Sometimes, the French bird, with bloody plumage and broken wings, falls gloriously upon the sacred soil which it had come to defend.

"Over the city each vulture had selected the place for which its savage instinct had a preference. One soared over a church. Another over a school where innocent little children, gay as larks, were learning to hate Germany!

"With a guttural cry of gratified rage the black band disappeared on fleeting wings, harassed by the courageous pigeons.

"On the following night they came again, hiding their somber plumage in the deepest shadows.

"This series of misfortunes had to be stopped. But what was the power that could put an end to these assassinations?

* * * * * * * *

"However, on a certain day the city had the air of a feast day, though no one could tell why all faces smiled. The habitual gravity had given way to a serene tranquility. Hearts were light. A new life seemed to have been born.

"Upon what did this sudden metamorphosis rest? The rigors of a hard winter had not stopped the bloody incursions of the black birds. On the contrary, the cold seemed to have made them even more savage and greedy.

"Notwithstanding, this city in Lorraine, so long plunged in sorrowful apathy, suddenly awakened. Was the nightmare about to cease?

"The explanation of these strange events came one day in January. Snow covered the country, shining in all its resplendent whiteness under the pale rays of a Winter sun. Suddenly, throughout the city, what strange sounds were heard:

"The Storks! The Storks!'

"Then they appeared upon the horizon, a bright line advancing rapidly. They were soaring at a great height. They count a dozen. On long, slender wings they come slowly down and land upon a broad field, back of great woods which surround the city.

"The joyful inhabitants shout enthusiastically. The nightmare would now soon be over. These glorious birds, which avenge and clear the heavens, were ready for battle, now on equal terms, in which their skill and their valor would triumph over the ferocious robbers.

"On the very morrow the fray in the heavens begins. On that very day the two sinister riders of the Apocalypse did not appear. The winter birds sang over the plowed fields. The sun became warmer, its light brighter. Then the unknowing robbers came as was their habit. This calm quiet seemed to make them hesitate, as if suspecting a danger which they did not know. Some, boldly came closer. That was the signal for the hecatomb.

"From the skies where they had kept themselves invisible, the storks plunged downward, and in powerful flight, magnificently beautiful, they pounced upon the black birds, all surprised and stunned. The long beaks of the avenging birds would soon pierce the hearts of the rapid hawks or huge vultures. All of them were not to return home. Some of them, slashed to bits, were to redden the snow. As soon as they were lifted up they were nailed in the pillory in the principal square of the village.

"For several days the savages did not come back. The Storks went after them, to attack them in their own nests and vengeance was exacted implacably. 'Eye for eye, tooth for tooth!'

"The number of victims increased. The purging was quickly done. For a long time the city saw no more black birds, except those which, after being conquered, stretched their remains on the square in exhibition. The bad dream was over. The lesson had been as deserved.

"Several of the Storks in the course of these combats distinguished themselves particularly. One of them, already celebrated in the bird world and on earth, was named Guynemer. He was young and had not yet grown the plumage of the adult bird, but on the left side of his white garb there were many colors —red, yellow, green — the emblem of the glorious heroism of this splendid bird, who with pitiless beak had already brought to earth many of those black birds."

CHAPTER XVII
A First Triple

If at the moment of the Verdun attack the East had been unfortunate for the Ace of Aces, on the contrary Nancy was to be worth an entire series of successes, one of which was an official triple (felling three aeroplanes in one day). Nungesser was the only other man up to that time who had achieved a similar exploit, triumphing over an airship and two aeroplanes on September 26th, 1916. Guynemer, the hero of "Doubles," did even better, bringing down four enemies within ten hours!

He began his avenging patrols on February 7th at 11:20, over the forest of Bezange, bringing down one adversary, completely disabled. This was merely to get the Lorraine sky well in hand, we might say; for this semi-success does not count. Tomorrow the Ace will do better!

On this day the flight was a difficult one. Guynemer told me about it at the same time that he was telling of subsequent victories:

"I had left on February 8th, cruising with my comrade Chainat. Of course the Boches, who still thought themselves secure, did not hesitate to try an incursion over Nancy. But we opened their eyes.

"Suddenly we saw a tremendous machine, equipped with two Mercedes motors of 220 horsepower, carrying three men, scattering fire and bullets on all sides. It was a Gotha; an aeroplane little known at the time and very formidable. Neither one of us hesitated for an instant, but each attacked it from opposite sides. I felt easy with Chainat, for he is cool, brave, resourceful and deliberate. We soon ascertained that these machines have considerable dead angles of fire. In fact, we would have had to be very stupid not to see the points at which the bullets fired so profusely could not reach us. We fired entire belts of cartridges while avoiding the fire of the enemy and forced the aero bus, whose radiator we had smashed, to land in our lines at Bouconville, where the three passengers were made prisoners. The apparatus had been struck by 18 bullets.

On the day afterwards Guynemer probably beat down an aeroplane at 11:15 near Nomeny, for this was the famous day, March 16th. And as is the case in the greatest achievements, the purely anecdotic side of this triple is rather weak. In a few words the hero told me about it:

"Two in the morning in twenty two minutes, one in the afternoon. The chief point of interest in the story is that all three fell within our lines and that one of the Boches was a well-known Ace, Lieutenant von Hausen, the nephew of a general.

"I brought down the first one in flames, a two seated Albatros, at 9:08. He fell on the Foucrey farm, near the village of Serres. The machine was a cinder. At 9:30, after fighting against three single seated hunting planes, with Deullin, I was again fortunate, bringing one to earth north of Hoeville, the Rumpler

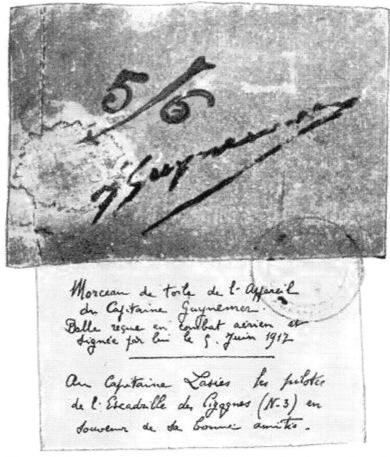

Piece of the canvas from one of Guynemer's wings, pierced by a Bôche bullet June 7, 1917, signed by him and given to Captain Lasies.

driven by von Hausen. Finally at 2:80 my thirty fourth victim fell to the earth in flames at Regnieville en Haye. This was another two seater. Five Boches were thus withdrawn from circulation, two Albatroses and a Rumpler, which the King of Prussia no longer owned."

Promoted to a captaincy, Guynemer brought down his thirty fifth in flames on March 17th, over the lines between Attilloncourt and Attancourt. A few shots had been enough to send this somber Boche into nothingness.

And an admirable, unique citation thanked the pilot in these words:

"On February 8th, March 16 and 17, 1917, he has brought down five enemy aeroplanes within our lines.

Only one palm for five enemies fallen within our lines in five weeks. Only a Guynemer could secure no more recognition!

The Aisne section was to have need of our best pilots and the Storks were the first called. It was for an offensive and they were to put out the eyes of the enemy. Our Boche hunters were to have work and glory enough.

Guynemer was hurrying the completion of his new aeroplane, built upon lines which would revolutionize hunting aviation. After a couple of trials he went to the front, went up in the air, beat down what he found and returned. Thus it was that on April 13th he beat down a machine and the second day afterwards he began again, but only the latter is counted for him, notwithstanding the certainty that the other was destroyed.

CHAPTER XVIII
Vengeance Is Stronger Than Death

An official announcement of May 8th speaks thus laconically about the Giant of Space:

"Captain Guynemer has beaten down his thirty seventh and thirty eighth adversaries."

The latter was especially difficult.

"That cursed thirty eighth," said Guynemer, "was one who certainly brought me a few sensations. I had attacked and thought that I had beaten him without difficulty, for I saw him going downward out of control. The pilot had been killed by the first shots, for I plainly saw his head fall over in the fuselage. Everything was going well and

I followed the flight chiefly to locate the spot where he was about to crash to earth.

"I paid no attention whatsoever to what was going on aboard. To me that Boche was listed, catalogued, numbered and dead.

"Yes, but we do not think of everything. Suddenly a hail of bullets swept around my Spad. That was coming it strong! I was showered on all sides, and it is a miracle that I was not wounded, or killed outright. A man has to watch everything in this profession. I looked and saw the observer, who was trying to deliver a second round. His aeroplane was falling through space, his pilot was dead, but he would avenge himself. And I must admit that this attempt was very fine; knowing that in a few instants he would be nothing more than a mass of mangled flesh and bones crushed to the earth, he was trying his best to take with him the one who had brought about his death. Yes, it was magnificent, but after all did not this Boche consider that his pilot was no more, and was he thinking of some manoeuver? I think, weighing the mentality of the enemy, that this hypothesis was a closer approach to the normal.

"Nevertheless, I shall always remember that adversary standing up tragically in the fuselage and sending a fire at me that was indeed direct. Several important parts of my machine were struck, but happily without any serious consequences.

"Notwithstanding everything, I may be wrong in passing a rash judgment upon the observer. It would have been so noble, if true, had he utilized the last seconds of his life in trying to bring me down. 'Ave Caesar morituri te salutant' (the ancient salutation of the gladiators in the Roman circus) would in this case have to read: 'Adieu, Guynemer, he who is about to die, kills you. 'Some others, but Frenchmen, have done so. You remember that case of the tragedy which you have related about Lieutenant Floch and Sergeant Rhode coming down all afire and how they turned and charged directly at the Fokker which had beaten them, locking themselves into it, and that they thus took it with them to destruction in the midst of spouting flames. They were young indeed, but we can only bow before brave boys of such temper."

New citation: "Incomparable hunting pilot: April 14th, May 2nd and May 4th, 1917, he has beaten down his thirty sixth, thirty seventh and thirty eighth enemy aeroplanes."

And now we come to the most glorious day of all, if in this debauch of heroism one of them could prove more glorious than the others.

CHAPTER XIX
The Magic Quadruple

It was on May 25th, 1917, that Guynemer succeeded in defeating four aeroplanes, one of these in one minute. The official documents read:

"In the period between May 17th and May 31st Captain Guynemer has beaten down by himself five aeroplanes, four of them in one day. Two of these machines were brought down with an interval of only one minute between them, probably for the first time in this war.

"These five latest victories bring the number of German aeroplanes destroyed by this valiant officer up to forty three to date."

On September 23rd, 1916, Guynemer told me that he had beaten down two Boches in thirty seconds, but he could not get the second one made official. But now no hesitation was possible. Here is the Ace's timetable:

1st Aeroplane 8:30
2nd   "   8:31
3rd   "   12:15
4th   "   6:30

Here, too, is the press comment which appeared following this event:

"S. E. (Sein Excellenz) von Hoeppner has not a chance. Or possibly, to be sure of his words, S. E. von Hoeppner does not read the reports on aviation. S. E.

von Hoeppner is the Director General of German aviation.

"On May 28th last the German papers published an interview in which he asserted that the German machines and aviators were far superior to all others. But May 25th was a festal day for French aviation.

"On that one day Captain Guynemer brought down all alone four enemy aeroplanes, which brings the number of his personal victories up to forty two and gives his squadron 120 to its credit. These figures would be added to considerably if we were to include many cases in which aeroplanes were seen to go down beyond control, but where there is not absolute certainty of their destruction.

"Four aeroplanes beaten down, on one day by the same aviator, this figure has never been attained heretofore. On February 26th, 1916, Navarre secured the first 'double,' two aeroplanes brought down within our lines. Nungesser, on the Somme, destroyed a balloon and two aeroplanes on a single morning. Guynemer himself, in Lorraine, brought down three aeroplanes in one day. He has surpassed both his rivals and himself.

"He began with a double: at an interval of one minute, one at 8:30, the other at 8:31, one north of Corbeny (northeast of Craonne), the other at Juvincourt (east of Craonne), both the German planes came down on fire.

"'As to the French aviators declares his excellency, General von Hoeppner, 'they never engage in a combat unless they deem themselves sure of a victory: if they do not consider themselves stronger, they prefer to abandon the execution of their mission rather than engage in a struggle of which the result may be doubtful.'

"On May 25th, in the morning, Guynemer saw three enemy aeroplanes flying in concert towards our lines. Doubtless, one against three, he considered himself assured of victory. How could he engage in a fight of which the result might be doubtful? He pounced upon his three enemies, who took flight. He attacked one of them, maneuvering to get him in the line of fire, fired and after the first shots the enemy machine dived falling in flames.

"Meanwhile the danger for the single seated aeroplane was surprise from the rear. While he was attacking in front, it was necessary for Guynemer to watch the rear. Guynemer turned and saw a second adversary coming full at him, trying to reach him. But he had fired already from above downward, and hit him with an explosive bullet. Like the first, this aeroplane takes fire and goes down burning.

"The victories of Guynemer are lightning like. They require only a few seconds of fighting.

"Guynemer alighted after this double, but indefatigable. Fighting excites him, sets his nerves a-tingle and his will is made resolute. Once again we see him in the paths of the air.

Guynemer with the military medal and "Legion of Honor."

Guynemer and his machine, after a 3,000-metre tumble.

"Towards noon an audacious German aeroplane flew over the aviation field. Our squadrons have taught the enemy respect for our lines. The unfortunate fellow who ventures above them seldom returns home. How had this one broken through the barrage? But to ascend to the sky after him and to reach him, no matter how speedy the machine, takes several minutes, time enough for the enemy to flee, having accomplished his mission. For all of the machines had come down, all except Guynemer,

"On the aviation field everyone was looking into the air, some straining their eyes, others with field-glasses. Someone shouted all at once:

"There's Guynemer!"

The German was doomed.

Guynemer came upon him like a whirlwind. He fired upon his adversary. Only one shot from his machine gun was heard. The aeroplane fell, the propeller revolving at full speed, and dug itself into the earth. Guynemer had killed the pilot with a bullet in the head.

That evening Guynemer went out for the third time. It was about seven o'clock, over the gardens of Guignicourt, that a fourth machine, beaten down by him, fell in flames.

And as the young conqueror came down at sunset, he executed all kinds of figures in the air to announce his victory to his comrades, all the turns, and twists and looping's in which he was so great a master.

"What can be added to such praise? What is to be said about that day? What words, what expressions are to be used? We have not sufficiently eloquent words in our vocabulary to render sufficient homage to this master of mastery. He plays in space and space belongs to him."

But some facts must be added as a sequence to the official announcements. The first aeroplane brought down was a two seater, of which one wing was broken by the fall, and then fell into the trees near Corbeny. The second, another two seater, fell on fire near Juvincourt. The third was a D.F.W., also brought down afire near Courlandon. Finally, the fourth, also set on fire, dropped between Conde sur Suippes and Guignicourt. Add to this that on that same day Guynemer had collaborated with Captain Auger (the slain Ace) in a demi-success, and that he put to flight with the same pilot a group of six single seaters. Are we not right when we call this Ace "The Giant of the Air"?

CHAPTER XX
An Enemy Picture Of Guynemer

It is amusing now to read about Guynemer's tactics, according to the Boches. It was the subject of an article which seems to have been inspired by the German General Staff, for I had occasion to find it in several different papers. Here is a translation of what appeared in the Badische Presse of August 8th, 1917.

"That man flying so high is the celebrated Guynemer. He is the rival of the boldest German pilots, the glory of French aviation, an Ace, as the French call their most successful air fighters. He is a redoubtable antagonist, for he is the absolute master of his rapid machine and, moreover, an expert gunner. But this Ace never accepts a duel in the skies except under conditions most favorable to himself. He flies above the German lines at an altitude which varies between 6,000 and 7,000 meters, a height at which no aerial cannon of defense can reach him. His flights are never for observation purposes, for from that height he can distinguish nothing; he cannot even note the movements of the German troops. "

Guynemer is solely a hunting aviator who attacks enemy aeroplanes. In this domain his triumphs have been quite numerous, although he is not a Richthofen. He is very prudent in his attacks. Flying always, as we have stated, at about 6,000 meters high he waits until an aeroplane rises from the German lines or returns towards them. Then he swoops down upon him like a falcon and opens fire with his machine gun. If he succeeds only in wounding his adversary, or if this enemy, untouched, accepts battle, Guynemer takes refuge in the French lines at a speed of 250 kilometers an hour, which his very powerful motor makes possible. He never accepts battle upon equal terms. Everyone must hunt as he can."

To this monument of equivocation the facts cited before are a clear reply. But it seems to me useful to correct some of the lies or statements contained in this sad paper.

First "No anti-aircraft cannon can reach Guynemer." However, on September 23rd, 1916, our 75 anti-aircraft accomplished the task which the Germans confess they cannot do.

Second "Guynemer is solely a hunting aviator who attacks the enemy aeroplanes." If only M. de la Palisse were still alive he would not give any other definition of the hunter of Boches. But we recall that this Ace also knew how to accomplish fruitful reconnoissances at the time when he was not yet "solely" a hunting aviator. The author of this article ought to ask a violinist if introduced to him, "Please play the clarinet."

Third "Guynemer is not a Richthofen." Thank God! Captain Baron von Richthofen takes advantage of all kinds of bluffs and painful circumstances which often sadden the enemy aviators. The number of his victories rises like a thermometer in the sun whenever valiant enemy Aces fall, or the supremacy of the air belongs to us beyond question. We have to think that this Richthofen is not a myth, a fantastic personage who in himself alone represents all of the hunting done. That would be a useful precaution: in this way the Boches would not risk losing him. When he was cited for the first time in an official communication the Wolff Agency accorded him seventeen victories. But he had never beaten down an aeroplane. His perseverance in mediocrity had made him celebrated, but he did not know how to take the place of Boelcke who was a real fighter. Oh, no, the Boche is right a thousand times over: "Guynemer is not a Richthofen," and we congratulate ourselves that this is true.

Fourth Guynemer's tactics, so rigorously analyzed in the course of the article, are to be objected to only for one reason. These tactics were never the tactics of the Ace, but they were the tactics which made Lieutenant Immelmann glorious in Germany, gaining him the sobriquet, "The Falcon of Cambrai." There is, however, one little mistake: Immelmann could never take refuge in his own lines, for he never came over ours. In reply to this grotesque journalist, let us recall to his mind that pursuit for more than seventy kilometers, which resulted in a double victory for our hero on November 10th, 1916

Captain Guynemer decorated with the Rosette of the Legion of Honor, in the presence of the troops of France.

He has just received the Rosette as an officer of the Legion of Honor.

Fifth "He never accepts battle upon equal terms." True, for all the greatest German Aces were his inferiors and this is the reason that, being never satisfied with their quality, he had to content himself modestly with quantity. Lieutenant von Hansen, taken prisoner, would be vexed indeed if he knew how little his compatriots thought of him.

Sixth "Everyone must hunt as he can." There again we agree fully and it is well for them that there was never another man like Guynemer, because he hunted as he could, and whatever he wanted to do he could do. Among the Boches their hunters do what they can, but the expression can never be used with that same significance.

CHAPTER XXI
An Officer Of The Legion Of Honor

The exploit of May 25th was well worth the rosette of the Legion of Honor which was awarded to Captain Guynemer with this rugged commendation:

"An elite officer, a fighting pilot as skillful as audacious. He has rendered glowing service to the Country, both by the number of his victories and the daily example which he has set of burning ardor and even greater mastery increasing from day to day. Unconscious of danger, on account of his sureness of method and precision of manoeuvers, he has become the most redoubtable of all to the enemy. On May 25th, 1917, he accomplished one of his most brilliant exploits, beating down two enemy aeroplanes in one minute and gaining two more victories on the same day. By all of his exploits he has contributed towards exalting the courage and enthusiasm of those who, from the trenches, were the witnesses of his triumphs. He has brought down forty five aeroplanes, received twenty citations and been wounded twice."

The forty fourth and forty fifth victims were brought down on June 5th; one was an Albatros which crashed to earth near Berry du Bac, when the hero attacked a D.F.W., which after having given the signal of surrender, tried to flee, thinking that the Frenchman had his machine gun jammed. But during the pursuit this weapon did not remain inactive, for it began to work and did fire: a few cartridges and the aeroplane began tumbling through the air, throwing the passenger out as it fell, while Guynemer came down in the Forest of Berru.

I went to see Guynemer to congratulate him, when he made his first trip to Paris. He was so hurried that he could give me only a few hasty facts:

"What more can I tell you that has already been written about my day's work on May 25th? The official comment was based upon the facts as submitted by me. I could not help forgetting you under the circumstances, but you have already written about it in The Matin, Only one thing interested me deeply; to drop a Boche with a single bullet, the last of my belt, at the moment when that individual seemed about to come and defy us on our own field.

"This war has furnished me with varied sensations. My record up to that time was three shots; for on another occasion I had killed the pilot with one bullet and the observer with the second. Finally you recollect that one which I captured without firing a single shot, because my gun refused to work.

"Moreover, that trick came near being repeated for my forty fifth. It was precisely under similar circumstances, with the aggravation that the enemy had given the signal 'Kamerad,' and then tried to run away. Excited at his breach of faith and having been able to get my machine gun working, I made up my mind to be avenged. I was going to pulverize that Boche! While trying to teach those fellows how to live I have sent them to death.

"While we are on the subject of curious victories, write this down in your notebook. One day it occurred to me to amuse myself and at the same time to frighten a Boche by attacking him without trying to shoot, but passing as close to him as possible. I saw him, caught up with him, passed him, turned and what did I see? Was it because of an air eddy or fear? Whatever it was I saw the observer who was aboard the aeroplane make a tremendous leap into the air, as if shot upward by a spring and fall back, but not into the fuselage. The poor fellow landed all alone! I had time to photograph him with a special apparatus which makes it possible for me to bring back indisputable proofs of my victories. The picture is not very clear, you may well say, but we can distinguish after a fashion the agony of this fellow beaten down by persuasion!"

CHAPTER XXII
Eleven Shots For Three Boches

A few days later Guynemer was to present more evidence of his marvelous skill and inconceivable heroism.

On July 5th he dashed into the sky with that machine which the exigencies of the censor oblige me to term without greater precision, the magic aeroplane. It was really impossible at that time to say more about this novelty called forth to revolutionize the methods of hunting and processes of attack. It was the first time that the Ace had mounted his fantastic machine at the front. He was about to engage three D.F.W. aeroplanes, but he was not very fortunate. He had to do with some brave fellows maneuvering in concert and had to expect a vigorous reply. His Spad was hit by several bullets, one went through his radiator, another through his motor.

Guynemer went back. He had almost missed the solemn ceremonial which had been prepared for him. Yes, on that very day, when he had gone forth the slave of duty, to fight in space, he had upon his return to receive the rosette of the Legion of Honor which General Franchet d'Esperey was to give him. Such was the enthusiasm of this great Frenchman, for whom no respite, no leisure could exist so long as there was a corner of the skies to be cleared!

The damaged aeroplane had to be confided to the care of those admirable surgeons, the mechanics. Guynemer was compelled to go back to his Spad with machine guns. But this did not stop him from adding to his list.

On July 7th he arrived on the front, returning from Paris, where he had spent forty eight hours talking matters over with his constructors. He hardly reached the aerodrome before starting out on a cruise.

On the way he met a superb Aviatik of the latest model, driven by a 200 horsepower Benz motor. He attacked: at the third shot he saw it falling fast and on fire. This was very fortunate, for his gun jammed after the winning shot.

The second day following he gave combat to four single seated Albatroses. Three of them fled very soon, probably finding, as the official Boche journalist put it, that the "fight was unequal." The fourth received the full shock. The pursuit lasted while they descended from 3,000 meters to about 800. At this moment the Ace secured a favorable position: five shots and the Boche tumbled in flames in our lines near Villers Franqueux and dug himself into the ground. The cruiser went ahead. Less than an hour later there was another duel that was at an elevation of 5,500 meters. Three shots were needed to obtain the desired result. The aeroplane, a latest model D.F.W., fell with a tail spin flat upon our lines, striking squarely upon one of our cannon, which it damaged to a certain extent, at Moussy sur Aisne. The observer had been instantly killed, but the pilot by some miracle emerged from this drama with quite a sensation. He explained to those who came up to make him prisoner that his comrade and he had really had no chance whatever. They had just come back directly from Russia and the flight which had ended so strangely was the first one they had taken on our front. It was well worth the trouble of taking that long trip to find themselves face to face with Guynemer in space.

These three victories, the forty sixth, forty seventh and forty eighth, had used up but eleven bullets, for the very good and sufficient reason that the victor's machine gun jammed with deplorable regularity as soon as the fifth shot was fired. The Ace knew this, but he also knew quite as well that when he took the pains the least number of shots would be enough for him to conquer. He was satisfied to get all the closer to his adversary, an admirable precaution of bravery which illustrates once more the hero's character.

But illness prevented Guynemer from any more aerial battles for several days. He had to withdraw to a hospital, being the victim of the beginning of some kind of poisoning.

CHAPTER XXIII
A Modest Hero

Some persons, who thought themselves well informed, announced that the flag of the Aeronautical Division was to be carried by the Ace of Aces in the July 14th Review. But they knew him very poorly. He who blushed almost when any one looked at him, or when he was hailed as he passed, he who had a horror of ostentation and parade was not the man, no matter how great the honor of such service, to pass through the streets of Paris this way. He wanted to be unknown to the crowd; he wanted to be like one of those heroes of the infantry whom we do not know; he would accept, but he, Guynemer, would not like to be an attraction to the beautiful spectacle witnessed by the Parisians on the National holiday in 1917.

He spoke about it to me, a few days afterwards:

"I have seldom laughed as much as on that occasion. Many of the people seemed to recognize me and acclaimed me. My poor comrade who really carried the banner of the Aviation division must have been greatly annoyed by these ovations which gave him no pleasure. But he could not answer, 'I am not he!' And I assure you I would not have wanted to be seen walking along under those conditions. Why should I allow myself to be appointed when in the cortege the detachments of all the most glorious regiments of France marched by? Each one of those soldiers had done prodigies of heroism, each one was to be venerated and admired. How, then, should I have been picked out because of my activity in the Fifth Arm? Before such flagrant injustice I could not hesitate a moment. It would have been odious on my part to allow them to make me a banner bearer and to shout at me like the fat calf (the famous fatted calf of the procession on Mardi Gras). No, I would not have wanted to be merely the fat calf, at which they would look and say: 'There he is! That's he!' Not on your life! That is the way to make all the infantry detest the aviators, whereas the foot soldier and the pilots ought to love one another and live with mutual respect.

"Very often, when I have advanced these theories before some men, the malicious have asked: 'Why, then, do you go out with all your crosses and medals on your breast?' At bottom they were right, they could not know! If I do this it is not because I take pleasure in it, for if it be sweet to know that you are celebrated, glory is accompanied by many drawbacks. You no longer belong to yourself, you belong to everybody. To be well known is to see around you all the time a number of persons who never cared for you before but have suddenly assumed a pseudo friendship for you. All at once they find out that you are a charming conversationalist, an infinitely fine soul and more of the same kind of gush. Their object is to go out with you, and to take you to see their people. And when they look at you they imagine that you admire them. The misfortune of renown? You no longer know where sincerity begins, whether they are pleasant to you out of friendship or vanity. We are apt to become unjust to those who do not deserve it and confide in others who deserve it still less. The women roll their eyes tenderly as they look at you and when you think that they are looking at your face they are studying your medals.

"And the journalists! You at least have known me ever since I began, and my friendship for you dates from that time. But those who have only begun to discover me and boast about me because I have brought down more than ten Boches! I did not require any encouragement, for I had made up my mind to succeed or die; but, as to loyalty, did I not need words of cheer rather at the beginning of my career? No, you see, glory is splendid, on condition that you are a statue and yet ... at that very moment they pass by you without a glance and have no time to read what is inscribed upon the pedestal. Besides, which is the best known statue in all Paris, will you tell me? It is the Obelisk and that was never a man."

Guynemer's conversation was clever and youthfully delicious. When he spoke, the sincerity of his words was so plain that we dared not interrupt for fear of breaking the charm. He jumped from one subject to the other and it was only after he had finished talking about something that I reminded him that he had branched off suddenly.

"But," said I, "you have not yet told me what you answered that fellow who asked you why you wore all of your decorations?"

And now becoming very grave, assuming a serious air, with that deep look of his, he said:

"What I answered him? This: I think that I earned the cross and the medals loyally. Those who awarded them to me wished to render homage to the success which my valor or luck, as you please, allowed me to attain. I am the French Ace of Aces, and foreign governments have recognized me as such. I no longer belong to myself. Some may assert that I am merely a shop window, but it is a window over which it would be rude on my part to draw down the curtain. It would be like the person to whom you give a beautiful jewel which he shuts up at the bottom of a drawer. I consider that acting as I do is an act of courtesy on my part towards those who have decorated me, as well as an act of justice to aviation itself. My breast on the one hand and my officer's uniform on the other will remind every passerby that in the Fifth Arm there are not only coxcombs, always the same, walking up and down in Paris, flooding all kinds of bars with their presence, with ridiculous uniforms and tunics free from any decoration.

"I am the first to suffer the annoyances of publicity, but I maintain that I cannot do otherwise and that I am not less modest because I wear all my medals and my cross. You know that I have a horror of parade, you know my love for simplicity, you at least understand me, but how many there are who spread the report abroad that I am a swaggerer, puffed up with pride. I just let them talk, for it does not matter to me, and it will not affect either my mode of thought or of action. Moreover, you may be sure that, if they had as many medals they are the very ones who would have a war cross hanging far below the bar.

"There is only one moment when I regretted at first this exhibition of medals that was when I met a brave Infantryman, one of those heroes of which there are so many, whom no one knows. They have suffered far more than we, they have suffered anxieties, emotions which we do not know how to comprehend, and they are very inadequately rewarded. I was afraid that they might say: 'Those aviators are lucky, everything is for them.' But, no, that was not their thought and I took special note of the respectful way in which they saluted me. And that look they gave me was the sweetest, the most vibrant eulogy that I could receive. You may be sure that they know how to recognize the aviator who reflects honor upon the profession and the other kind. That is the reason that they feel not a bit jealous of those whom they have seen at work, collaborating with them and letting them see those beautiful tumbles of Boches in flames."

I can add but a word to these statements. I had written them down with the exactness of stenography. Those who knew the great hero may also testify to the same effect. That modesty, that sympathy for the Infantryman, were two of the most characteristic traits of his admirable soul.

CHAPTER XXIV
Victories Of The New Aeroplane

After having eared for himself energetically and rapidly, Guynemer hastened to leave the hospital. He was not yet perfectly well, but one great reason impelled him to hurry: the Flanders offensive! He wanted to take part in it, all the more now that the machine of which he expected marvels, and which had already received its very violent baptism of fire, was ready, having been fully repaired. The two convalescents, the pilot and his aeroplane, were to complete the cure by the aid of fresh air and murderous indeed for the Boches.

It was by telephone that the Ace of Aces gave me the facts concerning these last successes. He wanted to tell me that he had not been able to come into my office, because he had to leave again that very evening. The message should have lasted but a minute or two at most. Three quarters of an hour later I still had the receiver at my ear and a mass of sheets of paper covered with notes in front of me! When we talked aviation neither he nor I had the least idea of the lapse of time!

"You wrote in the *Petit Parisien*" said he, "that I got my fiftieth on the same day as my forty ninth, but this is inexact. I brought them down twenty four hours apart, at nine o'clock at night and they fell in the same neighborhood. For the first time I found out what my aeroplane could do: my two adversaries were pulverized and scattered through space.

"On July 27th I was with Deullin. There is a man of whom you can never say enough as to his courage and skill. He is an athlete in the full meaning of that word and I know few pilots who are finer and more resourceful. You ought to write about him more often, for he deserves it. He is not only a remarkable aviator, but he is a real soul, and this fact is sufficiently rare for us to point it out insistently in him!"

I answered Captain Guynemer that I had been desirous of showing my readers the beauty of the career of Captain (then Lieutenant) Deullin, for a long time, but I had been compelled to do so very timidly on various occasions, for I knew that it was very distasteful to him when he was taken up in the papers.

"Oh, of course," replied the Ace of Aces, "he has a horror of publicity. He is excessively modest and many pilots who have not half as many victories to their credit are much better known."

"But that parenthesis has deprived me of the story of your forty ninth."

"I was with Deullin when we encountered a 220 horsepower Albatros of the latest type, which soared over a patrol of eight other Boches. It had a most idiotic air. It seemed to say to its comrades: 'Don't bother yourself about anything, I am here.' And it gave itself such condescending airs towards these young chickens as if taking them to the hen coop. At least these were the ideas that occurred to me about that Ace, sufficiently an Ace to be placed as leader of so important a troop of aeroplanes. I came up from the rear, approached to within a few meters. Boom! The result was immediate; the machine was cut in two and burst into flame, the wings on one side, and the fuselage on the other. There was a general 'scatteration' and the great swaggerer was finally burned to a cinder between Langemark and Roulers.

"On the next day it was harder. There was some resistance on the part of my adversary and I shall long remember my fiftieth! My opponent was certainly an Ace. After a first shell which missed the target, I made a turn so as to reload at my ease and then come back to the attack, when the Boche with great address and coolness took upon himself to attack as if he were going to come off victorious and received me with a
volley which cut through a spar of my machine, damaged the rudder, the cowl and struck the exhaust pipe. My Spad was in evil case, but the first thing in my mind was vengeance. And really the man in front of me was a man and not a coward. Damn it, at moments like these a man must not allow himself to give way to sentimentalism. I fired! My opponent, who had a D.F.W., crumpled up in flames, like the one of yesterday, almost at his side!"

The débris of three aeroplanes brought down by the Ace in

Guynemer ready for patrol.

"How do you know anything about that story?"

"Isn't it my business to know all about every one of your fights? But they tell that story in so many different ways that I must know the real story from your own lips."

"Oh, it was very simple! I had just come out of a mass of clouds when I saw an English aeroplane some distance away. He came towards me and as soon as he was within range he began firing, I turned and twisted every way to show him my tricolor markings, but he persisted. What was I to do? I had to make a very rapid decision. If I dived he would follow me and possibly bring me down. If I did not fire back he would certainly 'get' me. I must put him out of commission. I did not hesitate any longer. Most fortunately at that time I still had my machine gun with me and without it what would I have done? We were quite near our own lines and by planning he could come down there, so I had to fire a few shots at his motor. I aimed, with what anguish of mind, pulled the trigger and waited. He had been hit and I saw him at once steer towards our lines. What luck that I had not killed him! I came down after him and as he landed I alighted near him and made myself known to him. The poor boy had been hit by one bullet in the leg, a few weeks of vacation, nothing more, but I never saw a man more confused than he. He excused himself so sincerely and vociferously that towards the end I asked myself if it was not I that had a bullet in the leg.

"He was a youthful pilot, who had just before brought down a Boche, a real one that time and he was so happy that he wanted to bring down everything he saw in front of him, without stopping to think about the distinguishing marks. Other errors like this are possible at a certain distance and several cases, more or less tragic have been recorded. It even happened to me one day, when I saw a group of aeroplanes. I came up to them to protect them, for I thought that I had recognized them as French. But they were Boches. There I was and I would not even pretend to retreat. They were five and I fought with them and put them all to flight.

"To finish with my adventure with my Englishman. It has been said that as a reward for my action they had given me the D.S.O. (Distinguished Service Order). This is absolutely stupid. I had received that high reward several days before this incident. This report is spread by those kindly gentlemen who wish it to be believed that I have been decorated not for my fifty victories, but for a mistake!"

CHAPTER XXV
Never At The Rear

One question had interested me especially, for I have discussed it in La Ghierre Aerienne:

"Now that you have your fifty Boches, don't you think that it is time for you to take a needed rest? You have shown what an Ace of Aces can do, but is it not imprudent to tempt fortune indefinitely? Don't you think that if you took charge of a school for teaching the tactics of hunting by aeroplane that you would render greater service to France than by remaining on the front? Would not twenty under Guynemer bring down more victims than one Guynemer? After the very hard campaign through which you have passed during more than two years, don't you think that a few months at the rear would do you a tremendous amount of good?"

"My dear Mortane, never talk to me about going to the rear, if we are to remain good friends. I would never consent to take charge of a school. Besides, I would possibly be a very poor professor and I think that I can accomplish far more by example than by precept. The preceptors are not the payers. I want to pay my debt to France and to try to lengthen my list of successes incessantly. Look at Ball, whom we tried to send to a school. At the end of a few weeks he became frightfully home sick for the front, and came back here. I am like him. And then, too, if the public hears nothing about me for some time they will say 'Guynemer, he has been caught at last!' Yes, at that moment they will forget my fifty victories, and will know only that others are fighting and that I am not with them.

"I know very well that I shall end by staying there. They always say with reassuring conviction, 'They all get theirs!' Don't you think that I have not thought of this? Don't you think that when I saw that poor Auger land on our soil to breathe his last in our arms after fighting with three Boches that this was not my first thought? But I have been waiting for this ever since my very first flight! I am simply trying to postpone it to the very last moment and to avenge myself royally in advance before I fall.

"There are some pilots whom you could never persuade to go to the rear, even to teach the students of our science. There was Dorme, who brought down one Boche a day and he was certainly one who would not play such a passive part.

"And then to be a professor—anybody can be one and they are often those who are least capable in the air, and yet can give the very best lessons. The proof of this is that hunting is taught the greater part of the time by those who have never really done any hunting themselves!

"As for me, as long as I am able, I shall be at the front, to defend my title of Ace of Aces. What, now that I have received all of the finest rewards, when I have nothing more for which to hope, can I ask for a post of absolute rest? That would be cowardice, you see! I owe myself to my Country. I used the most varied stratagems to get into the Fifth Arm, for I was resolved to be an aviator. I have obtained a position which compels me to set an example. To leave the front would be nothing less than desertion.

"And the Boches? They would be only too happy, and they would grant their Richthofen twenty victories more at one time to show their joy! They would say that their Ace had frightened me and that I had asked to go to the rear. No, anything but that—I shall hold on to the bitter end."

There was nothing to say by way of reply, no discussion was possible when he had made up his mind so resolutely. The high command tried to convince him, but in vain. The advice of friends was no more successful: one month later the great hero was no more!

At the conclusion of our telephone conversation, I asked Guynemer:

"As to Richthofen, I have had a project in my mind for some time. You know that they published the memoirs of Boelke, Immelmann and Richthofen in Germany. Their aim was to exalt their Aces and to depreciate ours. It was with a view to making propaganda among the neutrals and to increase the enthusiasm for aviation among the Boches, that they were published. I really believe that it would be a very patriotic move for you to publish your recollections. What do you say to it?"

"I understand your reasons very well," answered the Ace of Aces, "but I shall never do that work while the war lasts: even if the Government were to allow it, how could I get the time? Finally, even if these two conditions were met, I would not attempt it, because that very instant there would be a horde of people who would assert that I am pretentious and that I am posing."

"Let the imbeciles talk. But you must consider the historic value of the recital of your victories related by yourself, and the story of all your emotions while fighting in the air."

"That would be a fine affair! What could I add to what you know, for I have told you whatever you asked me to tell you."

"Yes, but that is not the same thing,

'He' or 'I'. Readers are much more deeply interested in a personal narrative."

"Never mind all that! For your 'Boche Hunters' I have pointed out two or three corrections of facts which were not precisely exact; for your article in Je Sais Tout on my first thirty six victories, my father helped you to complete the facts, and therefore if you wish you may make a study of me. I shall not stop you and am ready to furnish you with all the facts you may require, but when it comes to writing and signing myself, that I will not do."

Then we discussed a series which was soon to appear in La Guerre Aerienne, Alas, brutal death intervened, and we could only consecrate a special issue to the hero. And in the chapter of the "Boche Hunters," which he had read over, I was compelled to add at the close the account of his disappearance.

CHAPTER XXVI
The Last Flight

This was the last conversation that I enjoyed with the Ace of Aces. A few days later he returned to the front.

Once more the "Stork Squadron" was operating on the coast of Dunkirk.

The magic aeroplane which had been damaged again had been fully repaired. On August 17th the Ace of Aces brought down an Albatros, which took fire and a few instants afterwards a D.F.W. On the 18th he transformed a two seater into a torch, but too far away for it to be made official. Then he was obliged to have his machine repaired and resumed action on his old Spad.

On the 20th he achieved his fifty third victory, the last official triumph, a D.F.W., which crashed to earth at Poperinghe. These four days' fighting had earned him three more victories.

Here are the two citations dealing with his last successes:

"An incomparable fighting pilot. On July 6th and 7th, 1917, he beat down his forty sixth, forty seventh and forty eighth enemy aeroplanes."

"On July 27th and 28th he brought down his forty ninth and fiftieth enemy aeroplanes in flames; on August 17th he achieved his fifty first and fifty second victories."

A few days after his fifty third Boche, Guynemer took command of the Stork Squadron. Captain Heurtaux, who had come back to his post after Captain Auger, provisionally in command, had been killed, July 28th, was wounded again September 3rd.

Thus Captain Guynemer had the difficult task entrusted to him of guiding the Storks to battle. The administrative work, the task of looking after everything and everyone, did not stop the young leader from flying himself. He might have abstained, for his machine was still being repaired. But it was not characteristic of him to rest, even when he had a very valid excuse. He took up again his Spad with two machine guns. Unfortunately his weapons always refused to fire at the opportune moment. The Ace of Aces flew from five to six hours each day, trying to overcome his bad luck. It was a hard time for him, but he would not give up. Like the skilled gambler who tries to win by continuing his betting, he fought over and over again, but could not add a single one to his many victories. On September 10th not only did his weapons give him trouble, but his motor took sides with the guns. A breakdown compelled him to seek asylum with a Belgian squadron. Quickly he made his repairs, departed and returning to his own aerodrome took flight once more upon another machine. He was hit in the course of an aerial duel and had to come down again quickly. Another flight and more annoyances. His ill luck would not be conquered, to all appearances!

On the next day, that he might triumph over that which would not yield, that he might try his luck to the very extremity, he appealed to death itself.

On September 11th, 1917, notwithstanding the bad weather, Guynemer started upon a cruise with second Lieutenant Verduraz. After furrowing space for a long time without success, for atmospheric conditions kept the Boches on the earth, the two pilots at last saw a two-seater which appeared to be lost in the clouds. The hero darted forward, attacked, his gun missed fire. He maneuvered for position again without even trying to dodge the answering fire, so sure was he of himself in dealing with that young fry. What was a single two seater to him? It was not even interesting. But above all did he wish to bring it down, to turn luck his way, and break the long series of no results.

But what happened after that moment? Second Lieutenant Bozon Verduraz had gone towards other fights, with the conviction that his comrade would without a doubt, come out of the duel victorious, but he found nothing there when he came back.

Guynemer, the hero of dreams, had vanished in mystery.

This was above Poelcapelle that the career of the most prodigious pilot of the war terminated, after he had added up 755 hours of aeroplane flight!

We hoped for a long time, even after it seemed that hope was no longer possible. The Boches were dumb, adding the refinement of cruelty in not announcing their victory. The censor forbade the announcement of Guynemer's disappearance, but the news was passed from mouth to mouth. We thought that possibly he had been able to land, that he had concealed himself and was trying to return to us. The most impossible rumors were spread. No one could suppose that the great slayer of Boches could possibly have been subjected to the same lot which he had imposed upon more than a hundred of his enemies. Guynemer? Every one deemed him invulnerable; no one had any idea that he could be killed.

But many long days afterwards came the news from a German source. We could no longer doubt it. The Ace of Aces had been beaten down near the cemetery of Poelcapelle. Two soldiers had been present at the place of the catastrophe. One wing of the Spad had been broken. The pilot lay there, killed, with a bullet in his head, and one leg broken. On him was found his commission, which made it possible to identify the body.

The district, in which Guynemer had ended his career in a burst of glory, where he had by one bound leaped to heaven, was being hammered by the English artillery. Attacks followed. Our allies looked for his grave in the cemetery of Poelcapelle when they took it. But they never succeeded in finding it. We learned later that on account of the incessant danger the Germans had not been able to remove the remains to inter them. The soul of

Guynemer in the Great Beyond had the supreme satisfaction of not seeing his body defiled by his enemy.

Lieutenant Weisemann, who had committed the sacrilege of defeating this divinity of space, survived his success but a few days.

On September 30th, 1917, he who had written to his parents: "Have no more fears about me, I have brought down Guynemer and I can never again meet so dangerous an adversary;" he who by one of those tricks of fate which brings death at the moment when it seems farthest away, this Boche, found himself face to face with Second Lieutenant Fonck in the clouds. He was upon a Rumpler of the latest type and was flying around a squadron of eight aeroplanes which it was his mission to protect. The combat took place at a height of 5,000 meters. Very soon Weisemann was hit and crumpled up, struck also by a bullet in the head.

Guynemer was well avenged, and by that very one who, in his turn, has become the Ace of Aces, achieving the largest number of his latest successes while driving the magic aeroplane devised by that other greatest Ace, who will always remain such, even if the number of victories attained by him be exceeded by someone else.

The shade of the hero seems to lead the destiny of his successor!

The Boches, who cannot even show respect to the dead, revenged themselves upon him who had wiped out nine complete squadrons officially and more than fourteen if we were to count all the probable victories gained far over their lines. In a monument of lying and shame, which should dishonor its author, they published in Die Woche of October 6th, 1917, with the reproduction of the pilot's commission and card, this opinion about him whom all venerate so piously:

"Captain Guynemer enjoyed a great reputation in the French army, for he said that he had beaten down more than fifty aeroplanes. It is nevertheless proven that a large number of these returned to their aerodromes, damaged it is true. To render all German verification impossible, they have not indicated either the places or the dates of these pretended victories. Some French aviators taken prisoner have stated that his method was as follows: Sometimes, as he flew as the leader of the squadron, he let his comrades attack first, and then threw himself upon the enemy picked out as easiest; sometimes he flew alone at a great height for hours, back of the French lines, and then threw himself suddenly upon isolated German observation aeroplanes. If his first attack was not successful, Guynemer abandoned the fight at once. He refused to take part in long duels where it is necessary to give proof of courage."

We would not even try to refute such calumnies. We read them the better to abhor the Boche and simply shrug our shoulders.

We began these Recollections of Guynemer with that admirable chronicle devoted to him by M. Georges Clemenceau. Let us conclude them with equal beauty and piety:

"Captain Guynemer, commander of Squadron No. 3, died on the field of honor September 11th, 1917. A hero of legendary power, he fell in the wide heaven of glory, after three years of hard fighting. He will long remain the purest symbol of the qualities of the race: indomitable in tenacity, enthusiastic in energy, sublime in courage. Animated with inextinguishable faith in victory, he bequeaths to the French soldier the imperishable remembrance which will exalt the spirit of sacrifice and the noblest emulation."

Such was the twenty sixth and last citation, as it stands at the Pantheon, "The inscription destined to perpetuate the memory of Captain Guynemer, the symbol of the aspirations and enthusiasms of the Nation," according to the resolution voted unanimously by the Chamber of Deputies.

CHAPTER XXVII
The Fifty Three Victories Won By Guynemer As Told By Himself In His Notebooks Of Flight

RICHTHOFEN, notwithstanding his eighty victories as counted by the Wolff Agency, will never leave a name in history comparable to that of the two great heroes who preceded him in death: Captains Guynemer and Ball. The German was perhaps an able fighter, but by exaggerating his success unduly the enemy announcements have prevented us from considering him seriously, while as to his English and French rivals one thing is certain, that the total allowed to each is rather below than above the reality. Not to run the risk of error, it may be stated that Guynemer and Ball brought down at least a third more victims than their records show.

We have the good fortune, thanks to the kindness of the father of the Ace of Aces, to be able to offer some most interesting and authentic documents. They constitute a recital of the fifty three victories gained by Guynemer, according to his own notebooks of flight.

The first lines of the first volume of these notes by Guynemer are as follows:

Jan 27, 1915 Snow Duty
Jan 28, 1915   "   "

Jan 29, 1915 Meeting and Snow Duty
Jan 30, 1915 Extra Duty at Berloit Aerodrome
Jan 31, 1915 Extra duty at Bleriot Aerodrome

These five days, to tell the truth, give no evidence that the student pilot would become the most glorious of all. It was not until February 1st that he went out for the first time on a rolling Bleriot, for ten minutes. Then his training became more aerial and with a record of 90.05 hours of active flying, Corporal Guynemer made his appearance, June 9th, 1915, at the headquarters of the Stork Squadron, to which he had been attached. He had mastered all the tricks of aerial achievement and was inspired by a will which nothing could change. His girlish air made some think of him as a bit spoiled. He did not want to be so considered, but wished to prove himself a man. Very soon he showed himself heroic.

In the beginning he did a little of everything: scouting, signaling to the artillery, special missions (two as a volunteer: in this kind of work, two leave on the aeroplane, which lands at some appointed spot in the enemy lines, and the pilot returns alone), even bombardments and pursuits without results. At this time the squadrons were expected to render any and all kinds of service.

It was on July 19th, 1915, that Guynemer achieved his first victory. Here is how he tells about it:

"Left with Guerder after a Boche signaled as being over Coeuvres, catching up with him over Pierrefonds: fired one belt of cartridges, gun jammed, then got to working again. The Boche fled and landed near Laon. At Coucy we made a semi-circle and saw an Aviatik, at 3,200 meters, flying towards Soissons. We followed him and when he was over our lines we dived and placed ourselves some fifty meters below him, to the rear and left. At the first volley the Aviatik lurched and we saw the flash of his fire. He was coming back at us with a rifle and planted one bullet in a wing and another bullet grazed Guerder's hand and head. At my last volley the pilot sank back in the fuselage, the observer raised his arms and the Aviatik fell like a plummet, in flames, between the trenches. We landed at Sarriere l'Eveque. The Boches attacked us with their cannon. While taking the machine further I broke the propeller on a haystack. Left at two o'clock for Vauciennes, Vedrines piloting the aeroplane. Two hours twenty five minutes of flight, 3,700 meters altitude, ten minutes fighting at a distance of from twenty to fifty meters."

Encouraged by this success, which earned him the Military Medal, Guynemer went after more victims, but was not very fortunate for several months. It is true that the enemy aeroplanes were

Guynemer's favorite aeroplane, "Vieux Charles," on exhibition in Paris.

harder to find than today, and the guns jammed so frequently that you were never certain of not being made a prisoner together with your machine gun.

It was between his first and second Boche victories that the young champion performed his two special missions, the second under especially dramatic conditions. He notes them thus in his memorandum:

"September 18th, 1915. Special reconnaissance with Adjutant Hatin, Peronne, Busigny, la Capelle, Vervins, Laon, putting in at Pierrefonds. Two hours, forty minutes, 3,100 meters."

"October 1st, 1915. Special mission. Two hours, forty five minutes, 3,700 meters." Not a word more, which shows the innocence of this youth who, after experiencing so many varied emotions, might have written a few lines, giving his impressions. No, he never thought about the dangers endured, he was only thinking about the success which was to come.

He carried out several bombardments, one of which was important in results:

"October 2nd, 1915. Bombarded the railway station of Noyon from a single seated Morane-Saulnier. Dropped nine 75 bombs. Noted a very heavy explosion in the hangars situated on the northeastern side of the road. Made two attacks upon a Boche aeroplane, but he fled each time at the first shot from my gun. One hour, thirty minutes, 3,100 meters."

The next day he carried out two bombardments, both upon the railway of Chauny; one at 2:15, at 3,200 meters, the other at 2:30 at the same altitude.

And now comes a fight in which, to avoid the fire of his adversary, he placed his machine just below him until he could get his gun to work again.

"November 6th, 1915. Protection of reconnoitering. At Chaulnes attacked a L.V.G., 150 horsepower. My machine gun jammed (percussion spring twisted). Tried to fire at a distance of forty meters, from the side, then at two meters, underneath. In turning to withdraw I swept the right wing of the Boche machine. Result: a bit of my sail torn off, one ball over my head in the upper plane. One hour, 3,500 meters."

Another fight in which his weapon cooperated with enemy.

"November 28th, 1915. A hunting circuit. Attacked a Boche (at 2,000 meters), who defended himself with a machine gun. My gun jammed four or five times. The Boche dived some 500 meters. After reloading, attacked again. Jammed twice, the last absolute, an ejector giving way. Seven or eight shots at a distance of fifty to one hundred meters. Fired sixty times. Landed at Moreuil. One hour, 2,500 meters."

At last comes his second victory:

"December 5th, 1915. Circled the Compiegne district. Saw two aeroplanes at 3,200 meters, towards Chauny. I attacked the uppermost at the moment when he was over Bailly. I fired fifteen shots at a distance of fifty meters. The Boche fired twice, but I got below and fired thirty shots at a distance of twenty meters. The Boche went into a tail-spin and fell at 900 meters to the north of Bailly, opposite Bois Carre. Landed at Compiegne. One hour, thirty minutes, 3,200 meters."

He did not have long to wait for his third success:

"December 8th, 1915. Scouting over the strategic line Roys-Nesle. When coming down saw a German aeroplane high up and far from his own lines. At the moment he passed the lines at Beuvraigne I cut off his retreat and pursued him. I caught up with him in five minutes and fired forty seven shots from my Lewis at a distance of twenty meters, from the rear and below. The enemy aeroplane, a L.V.G. of 165 horsepower probably, dived, took fire, turned over and planning fell on its back at Beuvraigne, carried westward by the wind. The passenger fell at Bus, the pilot at Tilloloy.

Landing at Grovillers (47th Company). Two hours, fifteen minutes, 3,200 meters."

Guynemer now enjoyed a series of triumphs: on the fourteenth he achieved another victory, making three in seven days, at a time when aviators found it rather difficult to get their prey.

"December 14th, 1915. Accompanied the V.B. 108 to the bombardment of Hervilly. Attacked two Fokkers. One fell in a tailspin after receiving

Bucquet's fire and mine at point-blank range. Fought the second: one rocker arm shot away, one pipe smashed, one bullet in the propeller, one in the right wheel, one in the fuselage cutting a cable, one in the rudder. One hour, fifty five minutes, 3,000 meters."

It was on February 3rd, 1916, that he got his fifth Boche, and at the same time passed on to his sixth. His first "Double" was obtained under remarkable conditions:

"February 3rd, 1916. Scouting over the Roye-Chaulnes district. At 11:10 I attacked a L.V.G., which came back at me with its machine gun. Fired forty seven shots at a distance of 100 meters. The enemy aeroplane dived very sharply over its lines, smoking fiercely. Lost sight of it five hundred meters from the ground. At 11:40 attacked a L.V.G. (with a Parabellum) from the rear at twenty meters. He twisted and turned in spirals, pursued him at point blank range to 1,300 meters (fell three kilometers from our lines). I followed him until I lost sight of him. (This aeroplane had the usual yellow-tinted wings, the fuselage painted blue like the Nieuport and presented the profile of a single hull.)

"At 11:50 attacked a L.V.G., which dived into the clouds at once, where it disappeared. Landing at Amiens. Two hours, thirty minutes."

Two of these three successes were credited officially to Guynemer, the three necessary witnesses testifying.

On the second day afterwards came another victory, the seventh:

"February 5th, 1916. On the circuit of district Roye-Chaulnes. Attacked a L.V.G. before Frise at the moment that it was going back over its lines. Coming up to him head on, I shot upward. Fired forty five shots at a distance of twenty meters, after getting to the rear. The Boche lurched and dived vertically, giving forth a heavy black smoke (fight witnessed by Benoit of C-4). The Boche fell in flames between Assevillers and Herbecourt (seen by an anti-aircraft battery and by a group of artillerists commanded by Miribel). Landed at Moreuil. Two hours, thirty five minutes, 3,300 meters."

Here are the words set down by the Ace in his notebook, telling the story of two hard duels:

"March 6th, 1916. Circuit of Ressons district. Attacked a L.V.G. Several shots at a distance of thirty meters, seven bullets in the machine, piping cut, left upper spar hit. The Boche was able to get back. Landed at Estrees. Observer: One lieutenant from Pressange. One hour, thirty minutes, 3,300 meters."

As to the eighth victory, it is told with no more details:

"March 12th, 1916. On circuit Chaulnes-Lassigny. Saw cannon shots over Compiegne, cut off retreat of Boche (L.V.G.) He opened fire at 100 meters. I fired at fifteen meters, three jamming (an American belt of cartridges) at ten meters, fired thirty shots. L.V.G. went down vertically, on fire, and fell in front of

Thiescourt, 1,000 meters from our lines. I landed near the front, then at Estrees, then at Breuil. One hour, forty five minutes, 3,400 meters."

CHAPTER XXVIII
RECORD AT VERDUN

Second Lieutenant Guynemer was now called to the Verdun front, where the battle raged and where it was necessary for the supremacy of the air which had been taken by the enemy to be secured for us most absolutely.

But just the day after he reached there, on the fatal 13th, the Ace was wounded for the first time:

"March 13th, 1916. Verdun circuit, attacked a group of four L.V.G.'s, fired at sixty meters and missed. Supply of gas at Vadelaincourt. Two hours, thirty minutes, 3,200 meters."

Flew after a Boche squadron signaled as being near Revigny. Saw nothing. Circuit in region of Argonne. Attacked a L.V.G. Came up to within twenty meters on the side without having been seen. Turned to get below and was swept past by the speed of my machine; dived to reload. A quarter of an hour later attacked two Boches coming straight towards me. Came up with the first one of three quarters of an hour before. Fired at ten meters distance, looping to get below him. At that moment he also fired. The back, upper spar on the right cut in two, cable cut, right front standard of cabane cut (two blows in my face), windshield smashed, several bullets in the planes and two bullets in my left arm. I dived sharply, the second Boche firing and missing me. Good landing at Brocourt. During this second circuit a N.1104 with a turret, appeared to fire down upon me at sixty meters, a few shots with my Lewis and he dived towards his landing place without my being able to read his number. Two hours, 3,000 meters."

The wounded man was sent on furlough to Paris on the next day, where he was cared for in the Japanese ambulance. As soon as he could get out he wanted to fly again. On April 26th he made the trip from Issy-les-Moulineaux to Borget or get and return in thirty minutes on a thirteen meter Nieuport. His wounds did not prevent him from flying and he did not wish to lose training. It was May 19th that he again took his place in the squadron. He obtained a few probable victories, continued to add to his hours of flight to enjoy the health giving air, but did not secure his ninth official victory until towards the end of June:

"June 22nd, 1916. On the Peronne-Roye circuit. Saw a Fokker over his lines. Two hours, twenty five minutes, 3,300 meters.

"Peronne-Roye circuit. Attacked a double fuselage machine at ten meters distance. Machine gun would not fire. Got it working again. Dived behind him and made him go back to his lines. Attacked two aeroplanes over Villers-Bretonneux, set one on fire at the same time that Chainat did. Two hours, forty minutes, 4,200 meters.

On the very eve of his death, September 10, 1917, when the Ace was obliged to land at a Belgian aerodrome for repairs.

"Chaulnes-Peronne-Roye circuit. A two-seater which hastened back home. Three hours, thirty minutes, 4,200 meters."

Thus on this single day Guynemer had made three cruises: eight hours, thirty five minutes of flying. It may well be said that when he met a Boche it was because he was looking for him. The one which he had felled crashed to earth in our lines, near Rosieres en Santerre.

On the next day he came back from his rounds with two spars cut as the result of a duel with a L.V.G. Then he started again on another machine. On that day he remained in the air B.ve hours.

Another encounter which was so hard that the Frenchman had to render homage to his adversary:

"July 6th, 1916. Scouting. Saw a Boche twenty meters away as he came out of a cloud. No time to fire. Two hours, twenty minutes, 2,800 meters.

"Peronne circuit. Shot at by cannon. One shell hit a spar. About 6:20 saw a L.V.G. over the Somme at 1,800 meters. He went back almost to his own landing place. At about 6.50 surprised by a L.V.G. firing through the propeller. Engaged in combat. I went down to reload and saw the Boche dive down upon a Maurice Farman. Coming back to the attack I turned the Boche, engaged him: two cables of his right cellule cut clean, pierced his propeller. Landing near Chuiques. Boche snappish, but manageable. Two hours, thirty minutes, 3,200 meters."

So every day, every flight meant combats. The number of Boches never seemed to stop the conqueror of space. See what occurred later:

"July 10th, 1916. Fight of three against seven. Rescued Deullin (became a Captain, Ace with twenty victories) who was pursued by an Aviatik at 100 meters. One hour, twenty minutes, 3,600 meters.

"July 11th, 1916. Attacked a L.V.G. over Flaucourt at ten meters. Jamming. Explosion on board the Boche. His left elevating cable cut. Dived, but seemed to regain control. Forty five minutes, 2,500 meters.

"Circuit Peronne-the Somme. Attacked an Aviatik near Saint Christ, then a L.V.G. who took me from the rear, fired three fourths of my belt at between five and six meters. A luminous bullet went through the fuselage. At that moment Lieutenant Deullin fired a belt of cartridges from very close up, and beat down the L.V.G. Attacked seven Boches to the northeast of Peronne. Bad jamming at first shot. Two hours, 2,600 meters."

He had collaborated with Lieutenant Deullin, but would not accept credit for this one himself. He had scored an almost certain victory that morning, but it was not sure enough to be counted. He ended the day by attacking seven Boches. This was Guynemer. He could not expend his great fighting soul in any day's work. On the fifteenth he brought down his tenth Boche.

"July 15th, 1916. On Somme circuit. Brought down a L.V.G. (the wheels in the air), at the same time with Heurtaux (who became Captain after twenty one victories, having been severely wounded twice). Fifty minutes, 1,800 meters."

Three days later he was working with the English aviators.

"July 18th, 1916. Somme circuit. Followed three L.V.G.'s for an hour and a quarter along the Somme. Fought these three L.V.G.'s and some Aviatiks with some Havilands. 'Peppered' one of them to rescue an Englishman, then an L.V.G. Two hours, thirty minutes, 3,500 meters."

The hero's enthusiasm never subsided for an instant. His flying notebook is the most complete proof of what energy and courage, directed by an iron will and an implacable desire to conquer, can accomplish:

"July 27th, 1916. Scouting along the army front. Fight with a group of three L.V.G.'s at 150 meters north of Peronne without result. One hour, fifty five minutes."

"On the circuit of the army front. Attacked between 1,100 and 4,000 meters several groups of from three to ten machines, some of them with two motors and three seats. Surprised a double motor pursuing a Nieuport, which made a half turn. Attacked from the front at from 400 to eighty meters a double motor pursuing an Englishman. The Boche tried to fire back, but dived before he could shoot and was then pursued by Heurtaux. He dived once more without firing, seemed seriously wounded, especially the passengers. Fight ended in the Combles district. Two hours, fifteen minutes."

On the next day, a day of victory:

"July 28th, 1916. Scouting along army front. Attacked a group of four enemy aeroplanes and forced one of them to the earth. Attacked a second group of four aeroplanes which scattered at once. Selected one of the hunting aeroplanes and fired about 250 shots at him. The Boche dived sharply, seeming hit. Machine smashed.

Confirmation by English headquarters. At the last shots fired by the Wickers, a blade of my propeller was shattered by the bullets. The unbalanced motor struck its own machine, breaking it badly. Landed by gliding at aerodrome of Chepilly, without accident. One hour, forty five minutes."

This eleventh victory earned him his tenth citation with which Guynemer closed the first of his notebooks. It sums up thus:

Hours of Apprenticeship 90 hours, 5 minutes

Flight At the Front 348 hours, 25 minutes

438 hours 30 minutes

Aeroplanes brought down, eleven

CHAPTER XXIX
From Notebook, Volume II

The second notebook presents a different aspect from the preceding. The Ace is a man of action who detests writing. He is annoyed at having to keep account of his flights. He entrusts this task to a secretary in the office and often forgets to mention some combats. He is intent upon bringing down Boches, and considers these victories as only a part of the current day's work, so the facts are given even less fully than before.

The month of August from the 3rd to the 17th is not very favorable. The Ace is constantly in trouble with his machine gun. Just for a change, on August 6th, he goes after captive balloons. He attacks two, one of them three times, the other twice and forces both down. "Was violently cannonaded," is all he reports. On the next day he flew for more than six hours, but does not set down the length of his second cruise.

"August 7th, 1916. Scouting along Army front; saw two aeroplanes of the Boches over their lines five or six kilometers from Lassigny. Two hours.

"Army front circuit, attacked four enemy machines, cutting out one, but my machine gun would not fire. I made a half turn, received seven fragments of shells, one in the gas throttle, another in my union suit.

"Made the round to Cachy Chepilly and from Chepilly to Cachy. Attacked the German trenches to north of Clery in company of Lieutenant Heurtaux. I fired at the emplacement of several machine guns. After 120 shots, gun jammed, breech broke. Two hours, ten minutes.

"Just a trial flight."

That was a pretty busy day, but it added nothing to his list. On the twelfth, fresh difficulties:

"August 12th, 1916. Army front circuit. With Lieutenant Deullin attacked a group of three Boche aeroplanes, two of which were the so-called 'Bananas' and one an Aviatik. Deullin, whose gun jammed, had to withdraw from the fight. Second Lieutenant Guynemer continued the fight. Four jamming's in the first twenty five cartridges, then it fired normally. Two hours, fifteen minutes."

The secretary, who had the honor of filling out the hero's notebook, starts in the first person and ends either from admiration or timidity in writing 'I' by writing down:

"Second Lieutenant Guynemer."

"August 16th, 1916. Peronne district circuit. With Lieutenant Heurtaux, saw a machine of Nieuport type, without the black cross, low over their lines. We attacked two Boches over Peronne at 2,000 meters. The one shot at by Heurtaux dived and had to land. The second abandoned the fight. I could not follow, my gun jamming when I was at point blank distance. Two hours, thirty minutes.

"Bapaume-Peronne circuit. Saw five Boche planes in the direction of Bapaume and several others on the ground within their lines. Two hours."

But against the strong will of Guynemer even bad luck had to declare itself beaten. On the 17th he gained his thirteenth victory and on the 18th his fourteenth:

"August 17th, 1916. Army front circuit. I surprised a Boche and fired at him from a distance of five meters. Two jamming's in three shots. The observer was killed and the aeroplane dived sharply, giving forth a heavy black smoke from beneath the pilot's seat. Then attacked two L.V.G.'s over Montauban, three jamming's out of ten shots. Nothing to report. Two hours, five minutes."

This victory embellished by many jamming's, followed by the words, "nothing to report," forces us to consider the extraordinary mentality of our hero. To him there was "nothing to report" when he had brought down a Boche, although his gun had been most contrary. Those are the risks of war which every fighter has to expect: "nothing to report." They must be met calmly, without anger, without regrets, without pride, without joy: "nothing to report."

"August 18th, 1916. Army front circuit. I attacked a Rumpler, protected by an Aviatik, some 2,000 meters north of the Somme. Fired two shots at 200 meters, pilot probably killed, machine went down in a tail spin and crashed to the earth on the western

His eighth victory.

border of Bois-Madame. The Aviatik fled. Jamming after two shots."

This is one of the fights in which Guynemer showed most clearly his incredible skill. With two bullets fired at 200 meters going at a speed of about 200 kilometers an hour against a machine traveling 180 kilometers an hour, he succeeded in killing the pilot and bringing down his adversary. Ah, his machine gun would not work for him, all the better, the bullets that do travel are enough for him to conquer!

On the 20th some aeroplanes were "probably" brought down, but they are not made official.

"August 20th, 1916. Army front circuit. I surprised a German plane over Bois-Madame at 1,400 meters, fired down at him as I passed at a distance of fifteen meters, saw the observer seated in his place. The aeroplane dived suddenly. Immediately afterwards attacked a second German plane which dived. Two hours, five minutes.

"Army front circuit. Saw a group of four L.V.G.'s in the Montauban district. I attacked an Aviatik, taking him by surprise, at 7:30, 2,000 meters over the Somme. Fired twenty shots. As I passed at a half a meter saw that the passenger appeared to be wounded. The machine seemed out of control and fell to the ground. About 7:35 attacked an L.V.G., firing point blank at 25 meters, received several bullets in the motor, tank, cartridge case, contusions on the index finger of the left hand. Landed near Flaucourt in a shell crater. Two hours."

To be certain of the result of his fire, Guynemer had come back over his opponent who seemed in a bad way, so as to judge of the situation. He passed only half a meter away, to see the effect of his attack. The attack of which he was the victim kept him on the ground only five days. He began to work again on the 26th.

On September 4th, his fifteenth victory.

"September 4th, 1916. Hunting over Chaulnes-Peronne. I attacked a Boche towards Brie. I dived. I attacked four Rumplers accompanied by a L.V.G. and an Aviatik. I brought down one of them near Hyencourt."

Here are fights every day, two or three a day at least. And there are also some credits missing to him.

"September 9th, 1916. On hunting circuit. I attacked two Boches at 100 meters over Herbecourt. One dived suddenly towards Peronne. Pursued him from 4,800 to 2,000 meters. A bullet pierced two of my spars. One hour, forty five minutes.

On hunting rounds. At 6:30 p.m. I attacked a L.V.G., killed the passenger, then fired 250 shots at from 150 to 20 meters. The Boche dived suddenly towards the Somme. One hour, forty minutes, 1,600 meters."

"September 14th, 1916. On my rounds. Attacked three Rumplers over Chaulnes at 5,100 meters and another Rumpler at 5,200 meters. I barred a Rumpler from our lines for twenty minutes at 5,300 meters. Wind NW from 35 to 500 meters. Two hours, thirty minutes, 5,300 meters.

"Hunting. Attacked a Boche point blank. Jammed by a defective cartridge. One hour, thirty five minutes."

Read the account of this day and consider the amount of energy and self-control required for four hours and five minutes flying. When we recollect that Guynemer was tall, thin, puny (they called him "fil de fer", "ram-rod," when he was studying as a mechanic at Pau), that his weight caused his rejection five times when he applied, we are compelled to think that the breathing of the air at high altitudes is a wonderful remedy and I think that this is more nearly true that the Ace of Aces was a phenomenon of heroic will:

"September 15th, 1916. On the hunt. I attacked a Boche at 1,800 meters over Barleux. Jammed at the second shot at point blank distance. Attacked two others at 5,200; another, a Rumpler, at 5,200 over Saint Cren. The planes broke after a fall of 1,000 meters. He crashed down near Saint Christ. One hour, forty five minutes, 5,200 meters.

"Hunting. Attacked a hunting Aviatik, fired twenty shots while facing it. Attacked three Boches, firing at one of them from close range. He fired back (one bullet in my left wing). Attacked an Albatros, firing at ten meters. Killed the passenger. The machine seemed out of control, but regained the level after several futile attempts. Two hours, twenty minutes."

During this day Guynemer had taken part in six combats, brought down his sixteenth enemy and killed an observer, whose aeroplane fell out of control.

CHAPTER XXX
Six Fights In Two Hours

On the 22nd Guynemer did even better in the course of a cruise lasting two hours and a quarter:

"September 22nd, 1916. Hunting.

"September 22nd, 1916. I attacked four L.V.G.'s over Misery.

"September 22nd, 1916. I attacked eight L.V.G.'s over Chaulnes.

"September 22nd, 1916. I attacked twice eight L.V.G.'s over Roye.

"September 22nd, 1916. I attacked eight L.V.G.'s over Chaulnes.

"September 22nd, 1916. I attacked two Albatroses over Chaulnes.

"Six fights, two hours, fifteen minutes.

"Hunting. I was attacked twice by an 11-4 (aeroplane with a French marking). I attacked a single-seated Fokker biplane (tricolor rudder) which was firing at a Maurice Farman. I fired twice at a distance of between two and ten meters. The Boche fell out of control, but seemed to regain the level before landing. Over Barleux attacked a Boche who dived. One hour, forty five minutes, 3,000 meters."

It is interesting to note once more the various tricks of the Huns, who do not hesitate to paint the rudders of some of their planes with the colors of the Allies in order to deceive our hunters. So great a display of courage must certainly gain its reward.

Guynemer secured his the next day, but nearly paid for it with his life. Here are his notes:

"September 23rd, 1916. Hunting. Two fights at Eterpigny. At 11:20 brought down a Boche on fire, near Eochis; at 11:25 made a Boche land out of control near Carrepuy; at 11:30 was brought down myself, canvas coming off. I smashed my machine near Fescamps. Bruises (one bullet in a spar). One hour, fifteen minutes, 3,000 meters."

Guynemer went on furlough for a few days, coming back to take his place at the front on October 5th. By the 9th he achieved a "probable" success:

"October 9th, 1916. Hunting. Attacked a Boche at a distance of less than fifty meters, near Berny. He dived vertically."

On the 16th he shows his dissatisfaction at the close of the recital of the day's doings, all on account of his machine gun:

"October 16th, 1916. On the hunt. I attacked four Boches, jammed. I attacked a very rapid camouflaged single-seater. He could not fire a shot. I fired shot by shot, but succeeded in making the Boche dive sharply for home. Refused several fights. on account of the machine gun. Two hours, ten minutes, 4,800 meters."

More annoyances during succeeding days, but nevertheless no one was keener, no one took so much pains and no one passed more time in the air. And how many Boches might have been brought down, whom he had at his mercy!

On October 17th he found that he had to decline a battle against too strong a force, and this was on account of his gun again:

"October 17th, 1916. Hunting. Attacked five single-seaters. In the beginning had to fire shot by shot. At the end fired normally. The five Boches dived over their lines. Attacked a two-seater. At this moment, surprised by four or five single-seaters, was obliged to dive (four bullets in the machine). Fifty minutes."

And on the 20th the gun jammed at 8:45, just when the passenger in an opposing plane had been probably killed; another jamming at 8:55 when a Boche attacked from the rear at a distance of ten meters dived vertically, the passenger again probably killed; in the afternoon another jamming when a single-seated Holland had been fired upon from a distance of four meters, above our lines. The same thing next day:

"Attacked a single-seater over Barleux, fired one shot, the Boche dived. Attacked a single-seater over Barleux, jammned."

The beginning of November was no more fortunate, but nevertheless, on the third, a probable success was reported:

"November 2nd, 1916. Hunting. Attacked at less than ten meters. Fired one shot at a two-seater, jammed. Then fired ten shots, jammed, while the Boche dived over Bouchavennes. Over Peronne I attacked three other Boches who dived, and a

Walfisch, which defended itself. One hour, fifty minutes, 4,000 meters.

"November 3rd, 1916. Hunting. Surprised an Aviatik at ten meters, killing the observer. The Boche dived, losing strips

of canvas. Went down towards Bertineourt, out of control. Did not follow him to the ground. Two hours, 3,900 meters."

How simply and frankly Guynemer recognizes that an enemy gets the best of him:

"November 9th, 1916. On hunting circuit. Six fights with single and two-seaters, which dived. I attacked a group consisting of an Albatros and four single-seaters. Hard fight. The Boche had the best of it between 4,000 and 2,000. One hour, thirty minutes, 4,000 meters.

"Hunting. I attacked a Boche at Misery and another who had surprised Lieutenant Deullin at a distance of fifty meters. Two hours, thirty minutes, 3,000 meters."

On the 10th another "Doublet," making the nineteenth and twentieth victories :

"November 10th, 1916. On hunting circuit. I attacked without result three Boches, two of them single-seaters, over Roye. At 12:15 brought down a single-seater on fire to the south of Nesles (firing fifteen shots at less than nineteen meters).

At 12:25 brought down an Albatros biplane, 220 horse power Mercedes motor, in the ravine of

Morcourt. Boche protected by three single-seaters. Two hours, 3,900 meters."

This success brought Guynemer a fifth palm upon his War Cross. It was the third double blow achieved by the Ace of Aces. Notwithstanding the fact that the days were very unfavorable for aviation, he was about to add three more victories to his list during the month of November. Before doing so the hero had to pass through a trying period of storm and stress.

"November 12th, 1916. Hunting and trip Cachy to Pierrefonds. Severe storm. Flew over Noyon, the quarters at a height of 100 meters, the chief street at fifty meters and the railway station at ten meters (I could read the name on it) . Fired at from time to time by rifles. Fifty minutes, 200 meters."

His twenty first was beaten down four days later:

"November 16th, 1916. Hunting. Followed a Boche flying high over us, but could not catch up with him. At 1:40 brought down a single-seater to the south and be- tween Omiecourt and Bertain. Two hours, fifteen minutes, 3,700 meters."

On the next day he gained another victory but would not claim it, leaving the credit to a comrade who caught the Boche as he fell and finished him:

"November 17th, 1916. Hunting. I followed three aeroplanes over our lines, but could not catch up with them. They came back, and I brought down one. (Two hundred and fifty shots at twenty meters), on fire at the NW border of Liancourt la Fosse. Attacked while falling by another Spad. One hour, forty five minutes, 4,400 meters."

On the 22nd a fourth "Doublet" gained by Guynemer:

"November 22nd, 1916. On hunting circuit. Beat down a Walfisch to the eastward of Saint Christ. Surprised by four Halberstadts; received two bullets in my machine.

One strut broken. I attacked twelve Halberstadts, which dived, and then a group of three others. One, shot at a distance of five meters, seemed about to fall, another dived very sharply. Two hours, thirty five minutes, 3,700 meters."

This second one was made official through confirmations on the ground, and the third was probably downed, but was not made official.

On the next day the fight was a hard one, but fortune smiled upon our hero, who saw the death from very nearby:

"1st November 23rd, 1916. Hunting. Six fights, jammed when ten meters away from an Albatros. One bullet in the radiator, another in the back of the seat. Two hours, forty five minutes, 5,200 meters."

The month of December brought him two more victories, so that with the close of the year 1916 Guynemer counted twenty five Boches, official and at least forty in reality!

"December 26th, 1916. On hunting circuit. I attacked a Halberstadt at twenty five meters. Gun jamming after three shots. The Boche dived vertically, but lost sight of him. One hour, ten minutes, 4,300 meters.

"On hunting circuit. Three fights. Gun jammed when five meters from an Aviatik. Two hours, 3,600 meters."

The Ace had lost sight of the Halberstadt and conscientiously noted it, but the observers on the ground confirmed the fact of the fall, and made official this twenty- fourth enemy plane destroyed by him.

"December 27th, 1916. Hunting. I attacked a Walfisch at ten meters. Each of us fired about fifteen shots. The Boche cut two of my cables, but crashed to earth south of La Maisonette. Two hours, 4,300 meters."

This was the end of his twenty fifth victim.

CHAPTER XXXI
The Fatal Year

The year 1917 was to be the fatal year. Guynemer was to fly less than before, but nevertheless, in nine months he was to gain twenty eight official victories, that is three more than he had secured in all the time before.

Winter could not stop this indefatigable huntsman. On January 7th he gained a semi-success:

"January 7th, 1917. On hunting circuit. Nothing to report. One hour, forty five minutes, 4,000 meters.

"On hunting circuit. I attacked a two-seated Albatros at close quarters near Chaulnes. The passengers seemed to be absolutely 'knocked out.' After going down out of control the Boche straightened himself out. One hour, ten minutes, 2,800
meters."

On the twenty third and twenty fourth two more "Doublets" which allowed Guynemer to defeat his twenty sixth and twenty seventh adversaries on the first day, his twenty eighth and twenty ninth on the second:

"January 23rd, 1917. I attacked a single-seated Albatros and made it dive. Beat down a two-seater in flames near Maurepas. Made a two-seater dive, out of control, passenger killed. Made another two-seater dive, out of control. Having no more cartridges and seeing a Boche 800 meters high, over

Marceleau, tried to make him go down by 'persuasion'. At a distance of fifteen meters got a bullet through my propeller, cutting the cowl. One hour, thirty minutes, 4,300 meters. "On hunting circuit. Nothing to report. One hour, forty five minutes, 4,200 meters."

This account of one day's work is really one of the most glorious that could well be imagined. Two aeroplanes beaten down, two driven out of control and one more which the hero tried to force down within our lines by 'persuasion.' The twenty sixth victory was obtained at 10:50 near the railway station of Maurepas, the twenty seventh, confirmed by observers on the ground, at 11:30 in the suburbs of Chaulnes.

"January 24th, 1917. Hunting. I brought down an enemy Rumpler at 11:30 at Lignieres, on fire. Beat down an enemy aeroplane over Goyencourt at 11:40. One hour, 4,000 meters."

It would have been difficult to tell the story of a double victory more concisely.

Here is how he set down in his notebook the thirtieth victory, won on January 26th, 1917, his fifth triumph in four days:

"January 26th, 1917. Hunting. Made an Albatros come down between Mouchy and Compiegne by intimidation. The pilot when made prisoner, confirmed the destruction of the aeroplane at Goyencourt. Active fighting over Montdidier, Estrees

Guynemer's pilot-card, reproduced in "Die Woche," of Berlin, after his death.

Visiting card of a Bôche brought down by Guynemer.

and Mouchy, on Bucquet's machine. The gun jammed after ten shots. Two hours."

And now Guynemer was to go to Nancy to operate there with his famous "Stork Squadron." He arrived there on February 4th. On the 5th he had a breakdown which compelled him to land. On the 7th he surprised "a Boche at twenty five meters over Bezanges, fired fifteen shots, when the Boche dived, losing his canvas," but this was not made official.

On the 8th at last he achieved his thirty first over a superb Gotha, the first that had been brought down within our lines.

"February 8th, 1917. On hunting circuit. Pursued a three-seater over our territory and overtook it near Toul. Fired two short volleys and then a single shot at ten meters, because my gun jammed. Their left motor stalled and the Boches gave the gesture "Kamerade." At this moment attacked and forced me to leave on account of its fire. The Boche came down at Bouconville. Two hours."

On February 10th he killed a passenger, smashed the tank of the aeroplane he was attacking, which, however, seemed to straighten itself out at 500 meters from the ground and was going either to land or to crash down in the woods of Bessaincourt, making the confirmation impossible.

Meanwhile Georges Guynemer had passed to a captaincy. He was to adorn his grade in his own way: on March 16th, for the first time officially, he was to bring down three aeroplanes in one day, one for each stripe!

"March 16th, 1917. On hunting circuit. I beat down a biplane Albatros on fire near Courbessant. Attacked three single-seaters near Ebervillers. One of them dived sharply, wounded by me. He landed within our lines: Lieutenant von Hansen. Another took fire and fell, brought down by a Spad (Lieutenant Deullin). One hour, thirty minutes.

"Beat down an Albatros on fire within our lines, near Regnieville. Made a small two-seater dive in the same neighborhood. One hour, 3,600 meters."

The hero would not rest upon his laurels, for on the next day he achieved his thirty fifth success:

"March 17th, 1917. On hunting circuit. Brought down a two-seater, on fire to the east of Attiloncourt. One hour, forty five minutes, 4,000 meters."

While flying four hours and a quarter he had brought down four Boches!

From March 17th to April 8th, 1917, Guynemer went to the rear to advise with a commission which was devising a new method of arming the aeroplane which was to transform the machine into the "Magic Aeroplane." We cannot of course be more explicit as to details, for obvious reasons.

On April 13th he brought down out of control two Albatroses and on the next day secured his thirty sixth victory:

"April 14th, 1917. I attacked a two-seater, gun jammed, got six bullets myself. Forty five minutes, 4,000 meters.

"Hunting circuit. Attacked a small Albatros, brought it down afire over La Neuville (NW of Brienne). Saw six single-seaters, Albatroses, at a great distance. One hour, thirty minutes, 4,000 meters."

May, 1917, was to be the most glorious month in all the career of the Ace. It yielded him seven victories achieved in twenty seven days, but we must not forget that between the 5th and the 24th Guynemer was away from the front.

Here we give a careful copy of his notebook for all the period of glory:

May 1st, 1917. Buc-Bonne-Maison. One hour, fifteen minutes.

"May 2nd, 1917. On hunting circuit. One fight. Two hours, fifteen minutes, 5,000 meters.

"Hunting. Four fights, one jamming, but I brought down one Albatros of a group of four, on fire. Two hours, ten minutes.

"May 3rd, 1917. Hunting circuit. Wounded an Albatros seriously to the north of the Malmaison front. One hour.

"Hunting circuit. Nothing to report. One hour, thirty five minutes, 5,000 meters.

"May 4th, 1917. Hunting circuit. Two fights. I killed a passenger. I attacked three two-seated

Albatroses, one of which was brought down within our lines. One hour, fifty minutes, 5,000 meters.

"From 5th to 24th trying out my aeroplane.

"May 25th, 1917. Hunting circuit, four fights. I brought down a two-seater at 8:30, which lost one wing and crashed into the trees some 1,200 meters NNW of Corbeny. At 8:31 I brought down another, a two-seater, on fire, near Jusancourt. Together with Captain Auger, forced a two-seater to dive from 600 meters to a kilometer within our lines. No more cartridges. Two hours.

"Hunting circuit. Brought down a D.F.W. on fire at Courlandon. Forty minutes.

"Hunting circuit. Brought down a two-seater on fire between Guignicourt and Conde sur Suippes. With Captain Auger, scattered a group of six single-seaters. Two hours.

"May 26th, 1917. Hunting. During a fight my motor balked. Landed in the fields. Arose again. Brought down a two-seated Albatros at 10 o'clock to the west of Conde sur Suippes. Two hours, fifteen minutes, 4,500 meters.

"Hunting circuit. Four fights, one of which was against four single-seater Albatroses. Gun jammed. One of the single- seaters carried a No. 2 black gun, seen before at Nancy. One hour.

"May 27th, 1917. Hunting. While alone I attacked six two-seaters over Auberive at 4,900 meters. I forced all six down to 3,600 meters (three fights). Then attacked eight Boches, forcing one down from

4,000 to 800 meters, tearing off the canvas from my fuselage. He was taken up by a Spad and crashed down in a shell crater. Taken prisoner. One hour, ten minutes, 4,900 meters.

"May 28th, 1917. On hunting circuit. Attacked a two-seater over Bienne at 8:45. Attacked a two-seater which landed. Gun jammed at the second shot fired at a single-seater surprised at point blank range, painted white and black, longitudinally, in stripes about five centimeters wide. One hour, forty minutes.

"On hunting circuit. Two fights. Jammed gun. One hour, thirty minutes.

"May 29th, 1917. Bonne-Maison-Corbeaulieu. One hour, 600 meters.

"May 30th, 1917. Returned. Fight with four single-seaters. Gun jammed. One hour, fifteen minutes, 3,300 meters.

"Bonne-Maison. Villacoublay. Paris. One hour, 500 meters.

"Return. One hour, 500 meters."

Thus in the month of May, Guynemer had added to his list his thirty seventh, thirty eighth, thirty ninth, fortieth, forty first, forty second and forty third victims, of which four had been secured on one day, and one on the next day, an exploit never approached in French aviation. (Since that time Lieutenant Fonck, on May 9th, 1918, brought down six aeroplanes, two of them in ten seconds, passing from his thirty sixth to his forty second victory.)

Other successes only probable went to make up this almost inconceivable record.

The Ace of Aces was to fly very little during the month of June, a total of only twenty one hours of actual flight. He was at the front only from the third to the sixth and from the fifteenth to the eighteenth, so that in these eight days he accomplished all that he could. On the third he made a two-seater dive and killed the passenger of an Albatros, which he forced to land. A Boche attacked by him jumped into space. On the fourth Guynemer took part in eight combats, in two hours and thirty minutes, in various groups. He came back with four bullets in his aeroplane, a spar severed, and one control of his banking rudder cut. One of his enemies seemed to be seriously wounded. And on the fifth he secured another "Doublet," his forty fourth and fort fifth victims:

"June 5th, 1917. Hunting circuit. One fight without results. One hour.

"Hunting circuit. Attacked an Albatros at 3,600 meters to East of Berry du Bac. Brought down in our lines at 5:15. Attacked a D.F.W. at 4,500 meters, East of Rheims. In the beginning several Spads were in the fight. The Boche dived within our lines. My gun jammed when I was at point blank distance from him. At this moment the passenger gave the gesture:

'Kamerad.' I gave him the signal several times to land within our lines, but he continued to make off towards his own. At 2,200 meters I got my gun firing and sent fifteen shots at him. The machine turned over suddenly, throwing out the passenger and fell in the forest of Berm at 5:30. Attacked three Boches without result. One hour, thirty minutes."

In July four more victories, the forty seventh, forty eighth, forty ninth and fiftieth, even though at this time Guynemer was the victim of the beginning of that poisoning which was to keep him away from his squadron from the eighth to the twenty second. He took flight on only seven days!

"July 6th, 1917. Fight with five two-seaters. Brought down a D.F.W. at about 10:55. Two hours.

"Hunting circuit. Fight with an Albatros painted gray with red bands. One hour and thirty minutes.

"July 7th, 1917. Hunting. With Adjutant Bozon Verduraz, attacked four single-seated Albatroses near Brimont. Beat down one on fire to north of Villers Franqueux, in our lines. Attacked a D.F.W. which fell in a tailspin, flat within our lines at Moussy. Two hours, ten minutes.

"On hunting circuit. Nothing to report. Two hours."

"July 27th, 1917. On hunting circuit on my aeroplane. Went around with Lieutenant Deullin. Brought down on fire between Longemarck and Roulers a single-seated Albatros (probably of the latest model, very powerful, 220 horsepower motor) out of a patrol of six or eight over which it was flying at some fifty meters height. Fired one projectile and eight bullets at between five and twenty meters. One hour, fifty minutes.

"July 28th, 1917. On hunting circuit (my aeroplane). Brought down a D.F.W. on fire over Westrobecke. Fired two projectiles (20 and 150 meters distance) and thirty shots. Got five bullets myself: in the angle iron of the tail, in a spar, a strut, in the exhaust pipe and the cowl. One hour, forty five minutes."

And here are his last victories, reported in August, 1917!

"August 17th, 1917. On hunting circuit. ACES Brought down a two-seated Albatros at Wlasdos with my machine gun at 8:20.

Brought down a D.F.W. in a tail spin at 9:25, with a projectile to the South of Dixmude. It took fire at 1,500 meters. One hour, fifty five minutes."

Under these circumstances the Ace had used his special apparatus.

"August 20th, 1917. Brought down a D.F.W. on fire near Poperinghe. Two hours, fifteen minutes."

These are the fifty first, fifty second and fifty third Boches secured by Captain Guynemer.

Before his death he added some fourteen hours and twenty minutes to his flying time, but had all kinds of trouble with his motor and his machine gun. His other machine was being repaired.

On Tuesday, September 11th, the great hero departed on patrol. He never came back again!

"Account of Second Lieutenant Bozon Verduraz :

"Captain Guynemer left at 8 :25 on patrol with Second Lieutenant Bozon Verduraz; disappeared in the course of a combat with a two-seater over Poelcapelle (Belgium)."

Thus closes the second notebook of Captain Guynemer. These notes constitute one of the most magnificent chapters in the History of France, showing among other things, that the Ace of Aces had been in flight for a total of seven hundred and fifty five hours.

APPENDIX
The Action Of The French Congress And Senate

It has seemed indispensable to the completeness of this work to present an account of the historic meetings of the Chamber of Deputies and the Senate in which the Parliament voted the resolution under which a tablet was to be placed in the Pantheon to perpetuate the memory of Captain Guynemer.

The Meeting of the Chamber of Deputies held October 19th, 1917.

Adoption of a proposed Resolution to perpetuate the Memory of Captain Guynemer.

President: *The Order of the Day* calls for the discussion of the conclusions of the Commission of the Army, upon the request for the immediate discussion of the Resolution made by M. Lasies and several of his colleagues, towards the perpetuation of the Memory of Captain Guynemer.

The Commission of the Army has decided upon immediate discussion. Is there any opposition to this immediate discussion? It is so ordered. M, Lasies has the floor for general discussion.

M. Lasies: Gentlemen: Captain Guynemer belonged to Squadron No. 3 which was known to the French People and to their enemies as well as the "Stork Squadron."

This squadron was organized in April, 1915, with a membership of ten active pilots. Today it counts:

killed or disappeared, twenty two; wounded, twenty three. It has had six squadron chiefs: three killed. Captain Auger, Second Lieutenant Peretti,

Captain Guynemer; three wounded: Commandant Brocard, Captain Heurtaux, Lieutenant Deullin.

It has seemed to me fitting, that the voice of a friend whom Captain Guynemer honored with filial affection, should be added to the voices of his companions in arms and his chiefs. I ask permission to read two letters to the Chamber.

The first is from Lieutenant Raymond, the present Commander of the Squadron of the "Storks," one of the two survivors of its organization in 1915 :

"My Captain: Having had the honor of commanding Squadron No. 3 in the absence of Captain Heurtaux, kept in the hospital by his latest wound, I wish to thank you in the name of the few surviving 'Storks' for what you have done in memory of Captain Guynemer.

"He was our friend and our master, our pride and our protection. His loss is the most cruel of all those, alas so numerous which have illumined our ranks.

"You may well believe that, nevertheless, our courage has not been crushed with him. Our glorious revenge will be hard and inexorable.

"The great soul of Guynemer will often greet our cockades in the battle of the skies that we may ever keep aflame the fire which he has left to us!

"Lieutenant Raymond"
"Commandant of Squadron No. 3."

At the same time I received a letter from his chief, Commandant Brocard, who was the leader of that hunting-group:

"My dear Deputy and Comrade:

"I am greatly moved by the thought which you have conceived of consecrating the glory of Captain Guynemer by demanding that the Country accord to him the honors of the Pantheon.

"All of us have dreamed about this, struck by the idea that its cupola alone spread widely enough to shelter such wings.

"The poor boy fell with his face to the enemy, struck by a bullet in the head, at the height of his triumph.

"He had sworn to me a few days before that the Germans would never get him alive.

"His heroic fall is no more glorious in deed than the death of the artillerist fallen over his cannon, of the infantryman killed in the charge, or that more lugubrious death of the soldier engulfed in the swamp.

"But for more than two years every one saw him cleaving the skies, whether illumined by the bright sun, or overcast by somber tempests, bearing upon his poor wings a part of their dreams, of their faith in success and all the confidence and hope of their hearts.

"It was for them, for the sappers, the artillerists, the infantrymen, that he fought with all the rancor of his hatred, all the audacity of his youth, all the joy of his triumphs.

"Certain that the struggle would be fatal to him, but sure that on board his war-bird he would save thousands of lives, seeing combatants like himself born in his own image, he remained faithful to his destiny, faithful in the sacrifices which he made long before and which he saw coming calmly.

"A modest soldier, but conscious of the greatness of his part, he had the fine qualities of the soil which he so well defended, the tenacity, the perseverance in effort, the unconsciousness of danger, to which he added the frankest and most generous of hearts.

"His short life knew neither regrets, sufferings nor disillusions.

"Coming from the lyceum where he was learning the history of France, he left it only to write one more page in it; he went to the war, his willing eyes fixed upon his aim, urged on by I know not what mysterious force, which I respected, as we respect the dead or genius.

"Guynemer was merely a powerful idea in a very frail body and I lived near him with the secret sorrow of knowing that someday the idea would slay its container.

"Sir Deputy, ask that the Pantheon be his last home, where they have already placed mothers and children.

"His protecting wings will not be out of place there, and beneath the dome where those who have given us our patrimony sleep, they will be a symbol of those who have guarded it for us.

"Commandant Brocard."

Gentlemen: For three years, our army, faithfully supported by our allies, has written pages which will stand as the admiration and astonishment of history.

To our soldiers of all ranks, of all arms, and at this moment my mind flies especially to those hidden heroes of the common trench whose poor remains scattered by shells have neither tomb nor cross to which those who weep may come and mourn; to all, infantry, artillery, cavalry, aviators and engineers there is but one "Name" which can symbolize the grandeur of their sacrifice.

We select the name of this child who, in unforgettable prowess flew above our battle front, that land of France all soaked in blood and glory, of which the least drop would suffice to efface the pitiable individual failings which we have to deplore.

The homage which we render to Guynemer is homage rendered to the most heroic of armies and also to the most stoical of Nations by a Parliament which, I have the courage to state, has, for three years, made every effort to prove itself worthy of both.

Gentlemen, let us stop an instant and by a unanimous vote, answer that great voice of the dead, from the tombs and the air, which we hear always, by a proud Hallelujah of hope and victory.

President: The reporter for the Commission has the floor.

M. Henry Pate, the Reporter: Gentlemen, the Commission of the Army asks you to adopt the proposition of our honorable colleague, M. Lasies, a proposition to which it has given unanimous consent.

In the person of Captain Guynemer, whose career M. Lasies has presented with so much power, in the person, I may say of the "Ace of Aces," that most beloved and popular soldier, your Army Commission, like yourselves, wishes to glorify all of the warriors who for more than three years have fought with such heroism and abnegation and all of the obscure heroes who have fallen for their country.

It is proper to combine for this homage all the workers at the rear, who have labored zealously in all departments to insure the advance of the armies, those workmen in the factories, who ceaselessly forge the arms of victory; in a word, all the Nation, gentlemen, which has set a fine example of patience, calmness and courage, virtues more needed than ever before in these troublous times through which we are passing.

The proposition which we have the honor of submitting to you is one of those which requires no lengthy discussion: we ask that it be adopted by acclamation.

I have stated in my report all that was necessary; I have told of all the glory and all the courage manifested by that youth, that hero of whom we fashion a symbol today. The name of Guynemer will be in its proper place in the Pantheon, and in the "Gold Book" which we shall institute if we adopt the suggestion of our colleague, Paul Escudier, his name will be the first on the list, alas too long, of all the citizen soldiers who have died to save their country and the liberties of the world.

President: The Under Secretary of State has the floor. M. Jacques Louis Dumesnil, Under Secretary of State for Military and Maritime Aeronautics

Gentlemen: The Government is in full accord with the proposition originated by our colleague, M. Lasies and which our colleague, M. Pate, has just reported out of the Commission of the Army.

Very soon measures will be taken for engraving the name of Captain Guynemer on the glorious tablets of the Pantheon.

But already that heroic youth who is mourned by the Nation and its army, has gone straight to Immortality, with the greatest of those who, during the ages, "have died devoted deaths for the Country."

The legend of his life is already woven into the unbreakable web of the History of France.

Tomorrow, by our homage, we shall honor his memory beneath the dome of the National Temple.

Meanwhile he lies beneath the vault of the heaven which he conquered, in that murdered and sanctified earth, of the trench line, amid so many of his brethren, soldiers of all arms.

We all join in the same homage: in which the shining glory symbolizes the aspirations and enthusiasms of the National Army, and his comrades in hunting, of the army corps, of bombarding, and all those also, the hidden heroes, sometimes even anonymous, who each day pay the supreme sacrifice for the recovery of the soil of their native land, die to secure the peace and liberty of future generations, and who, for three years, have bequeathed their grief, and glory to France, enriching it with the most magnificent treasure of honor ever possessed by any land.

Guynemer has fallen; but his wings are not broken and already through the same paths in the skies, they are leading to victory all that shining Pleiad of those who would avenge their youthful leader and comrade.

The acknowledgment of all the country will perpetuate the name of Guynemer and raise his example to lofty heights.

May it be permitted me, today, in bringing him the highest homage of the Government of the Republic, simply to read the two last citations given this hero. They sum up all the noble life of this twenty three year old Captain, radiated by youth and honor.

Here they are. Gentlemen. One is the citation of June, 1917, when he was made an Officer of the Legion of Honor :

"An elite officer, a fighting pilot as skillful as audacious. He has rendered glowing service to the Country, both by the number of his victories and the daily example which he has set of burning ardor and even greater mastery increasing from day to day. Unconscious of danger, on account of his sureness of method and precision of manoeuvers he has become the most redoubtable of all to the enemy. On May 25th, 1917, he accomplished one of his most brilliant exploits, beating down two enemy aeroplanes in one minute, and gaining two more victories on the same day. By all of his exploits he has contributed towards exalting the courage and enthusiasm of those who, from the trenches, were the witnesses of his triumphs. He has brought down forty-five aeroplanes, received twenty citations and been wounded twice."

And now here is that very beautiful Citation by which the chief of the army in whose ranks he fought, only a few days ago, has summed up, I may say, all the career of this soldier :

General Order of October 16th, 1917

"The General commanding the First Army cites in the order of the army. Captain Guynemer, commandant of Squadron No. 3.

"Died on the field of honor, September 11th, 1917. A hero of legendary power fell under the open heavens of glory, after three years of hard fighting. He will long remain the purest symbol of the race.

"Of indomitable tenacity, boundless energy, sublime courage. Animated by a moving faith in victory, he has bequeathed to the French soldier an imperishable legacy of recollections which will raise high the spirit of sacrifice and bring forth the noblest emulation."

Gentlemen, I have ordered that, tomorrow, Saturday, October 20th, in all the aviation schools of France, to the four corners of our territory, homage is to be rendered to Captain Guynemer, at the same hour, before the troops, before those who are now preparing to follow in his footsteps. I believe that thus we shall honor most highly the memory of him whom we all mourn, and that no lesson could be grander.

I wish to state to the Chamber that, in order to arm our aerial fleet to the maximum no effort will be relaxed, no negligence will be tolerated, and all routine will be broken.

And this will be another way of rendering homage to the memory of Captain Guynemer.

More and more every day the most powerful methods are being employed so that our aviation may dominate the enemy and have absolute mastery of the air, which I profoundly believe will at the decisive time be an essential condition of victory.

President: Does anyone else wish the floor for general discussion? I ask the Chamber if it wishes to go from discussion to specific action.

(Being decided so to do.)

President : Specific Action. The Chamber asks the Government to have placed in the Pantheon an inscription intended to perpetuate the memory of Captain Guynemer, as a symbol of the aspirations and enthusiasm of the Army of the Nation."
Does anyone wish the floor? I shall put the question.

(The Deputies all rise.)

The resolution is adopted unanimously.
Record of the Meeting of the Senate, October 25th, 1917.
Adoption of a proposed Resolution in Honor of Captain Guynemer.
President: I have received from Messrs. Gaston, Menier, Clemenceau, and others a proposition of a Resolution in the following terms:
"The Senate: Joining in the homage rendered by the Government and the Chamber of Deputies to glorify the memory of Captain Guynemer, the hero of the air, by an inscription in the Pantheon.
"In him salutes the spirit of sacrifice, self-denial and energy of all the combatants in the armies of the

Republic, who for three years have fallen for their native Land."

M. Gaston Menier asks for immediate action on his proposition and its return to the Army Commission. According to the rule, I shall present this to the Senate, at the close of the meeting. (Voices — Now, Now.)

M. Paul Strauss: Such a proposition should be considered at once.

Several Senators: "We request immediate action"!

President: If there is no objection, we shall take it up immediately (Unanimous) .

President: I shall ask for a vote. The proposition is sent to the Army Commission.

M. Gaston Menier: The Army Commission having examined the proposed resolution, and has instructed me to present it in its name.

Gentlemen: On October 19th, 1917, the Chamber of Deputies voted unanimously and by acclamation the proposal of the following resolution, which had been presented by M. Lasies and his colleagues :

"The Chamber asks the Government to have placed in the Pantheon an inscription intended to perpetuate the memory of Captain Guynemer, as a symbol of the aspirations and enthusiasm of the Army of the Nation."

The Government, through Under Secretary of State J. L. Dumesnil, offers its warmest support of the project and approves it, the resolution of the Senate reading as follows :

"The Senate: Joining in the homage rendered by the Government and the Chamber of Deputies to glorify the memory of Captain Guynemer, the hero of the air, by an inscription in the Pantheon to his memory.

"Who is there among us," said M. Menier, "who has not admired more and more every day, the prowess of that young and glorious aviator, Georges Guynemer, whose renown spread so quickly all over the world? Who of us, while reading the news of the aviators has not trembled at times when considering his tremendous triumphs?

"Who, then, was this Guynemer, whose reputation was made so glorious and so quickly? Guynemer was a child of France, frail and delicate, who recovering twice from severe attacks upon his constitution, tried in vain to be accepted when he came from college. He was nineteen years old. After many attempts he at last succeeded in gaining admittance as a mechanic apprentice in an aviation school. He was already dreaming of great things, and if he dreamed of aviation it was because he knew that in this new 'Arm' he would be able to utilize all that great energy of which he felt himself possessed. He foresaw its importance and development. He soon became the brilliant, invincible champion.

"He began flying in April, 1915, and at once manifested his wonderful will power. Great indeed was his joy when he gained possession of one of those speedy Nieuports with which he was to establish his mastery of hunting in the air. His first victory took place July 19th, 1915; he fought at Verdun with all his might and from victory upon victory his name flew to all lips. But he was wounded. Scarce was he better before he was fighting again. He became Second Lieutenant, and without respite, he brought new glory daily to the famous 'Stork Squadron,' the celebrated No. 3. On one day he brought down four aeroplanes, but with all his triumphs he was still charmingly modest. His rewards came rapidly. His palms were no longer counted. He was named as a Chevalier, then as an officer of the Legion of Honor and then, see him Captain at twenty two!

"This timid young man, but so resolute, expressed daily the cold resolve to win; his youthful face became an aureole which the crowd admired and his example inspired the numerous experts who all loved him and were never jealous of his triumphs.

He had just achieved his fifty third victory and, a few days before he returned to the front, the signer of this report had the honor to talk with him in the midst of his friends. We said to him: "Stop a moment, you must not tempt fate forever, we need you for our victory." But he answered us, resolutely:

"My place is at the front, always in front. I have been brought down seven times, and I have always been able to escape ; I am going back there! "

"He did as he had said and only a few days later we heard with anguish that he had disappeared in the course of a combat beyond our lines. We hoped, nevertheless, not- withstanding the cruel impression left by that awful word, 'disappeared,' which too many of us have learned to understand.

"Alas, that last engagement was to be fatal, for an implacable bullet struck him in the head when he was 700 meters in the air, blotting him out forever!

"You have seen in the report from the other Assembly the letters from his comrades and his chiefs, his citations. Poor, but glorious son of France! He has deserved much from his Country. If his body has fallen, shrouded in his aeroplane, upon that soil of Flanders, already besprinkled with so much blood, his pure spirit has remained in the highest heights of the blue heavens and his fine example, ardently followed by his comrades, proves that he remains forever alive in the heart of each one of them.

"But, Gentlemen, if we thus celebrate the glory of Guynemer, it is because we take him as the symbol of our race, with his beautiful bravery, his resolute courage and his valiant energy.

"Our homage personifies in his name the prodigies accomplished by all his competitors and by all the combatants, young or old, by all those heroes, too often remaining unknown and who, like he, simply did their duty and fell for France. To all of them our acknowledgments go forth.

"But acknowledgments are not enough. It is necessary that the example of valiant Guynemer serve us by bringing home to us absolutely the conviction of the necessity for victory in the air without which we cannot secure victory upon the ground.

"We must be inspired by the prodigies which he performed to judge of the importance which should be attached to aviation in all its forms. The example of Guynemer will beget pilots; it is for us to raise up the machines which will give them power and the mastery. For this reason we may appreciate all of the acknowledgments which we owe to Captain Guynemer, whose example has served us splendidly towards hastening the hour of victory.

"Gentlemen, your Army Commission proposes the unanimous adoption of the resolution which it has offered.

"Gentlemen, I have said to you that Guynemer was a symbol and an example. He is really a symbol, because he incarnated all of the qualities of our race, audacity, intrepidity, tenacity, perseverance in effort and throughout all confidence and hope. He was an example, because the consciousness of having done his duty, nobly, without ostentation, or pomp, with an energy which never relaxed, allows us to see that he offered to his Country the sacrifice of his life.

"Permit me to add, in closing, that in the midst of the disappearance of so many of our youths, of so many deeds of courage, known and unknown, done by our incomparable Poilus who have done their duty so grandly and simply, the face of Captain Guynemer planes in a heaven of apotheosis. We see him in that glowing ride, dominating space, showing with his speedy, mobile aeroplane, the direction of the whirlwinds of battle and the combats behind which little by little the sun of victory rises, which he never was to see, but for which he had made the way.

"His glory is pure and truly French; as we write his name upon the cupola of the Pantheon, we are writing one more brilliant page in the glory and grandeur of our France."

M. J. L. Dumesnil, Under Secretary of State for Aviation:

Gentlemen: In asking the Government to inscribe the name of Captain Guynemer on the vault of the Pantheon, the Senate is certainly the interpreter of unanimous France.

Dead in the broad heaven of glory and this is his last citation:

"Brother of Assas, of Marceau, of Hoche, he has bequeathed his glory to his country; he has also bequeathed to it a great hope, and his native land, through the generations still to be, will immortalize the recollection of one of its finest soldiers of victory."

The resolution was passed unanimously, amid wild applause. Finally the Minister of Public Instruction and the Fine Arts, so as to connect the youth of France with the national homage rendered to the hero and his companions in arms, addressed an order to all scholastic establishments requiring all principals, directors and heads of colleges of every kind, to read to all of the pupils, while standing at attention, the resolution of the Chamber of Deputies, which decided that the name of Captain Guynemer was to be inscribed upon the walls of the Pantheon.

In every corps of the French Army the resolution was also read.

FINIS

THE PHOTOGRAPHIC LIBRARY OF CAPTAIN GEORGES GUYNEMER

A Pose With His Spad

Albatros DIII defeat

Capt. Guynemer in Old Charles

Capt. Guynemer Age 22 with 50 kills

G. Guynemer working on Spad XIII S504

Georges Guynemer in Spad VII S254 with camera mounting bracket

Among the first French aces to fly the Spad 13 in combat was Guynemer, who was assigned Spad 13 (S.504) in September of 1917. Guynemer was lost flying this aircraft on 11 September. S.504 bears the Stork insignia of Spa. 3 (White with Back wings) and Guynemer's personal number, 2 on the fuselage side, however, it did not carry the name *Vieux Charles*.

Guynemer posing with enemy AA

George Guynemer prepares for take off from Belgian Les Moeres aerodrome following repairs to a faulty water pump on 10 September 1917.

CAPT Georges Guynemer in his third Spad 7 (serial S.254) on 25 May 1917. This aircraft was the first Spad 7 powered by the 180 hp Hispano-Suiza to be sent to the front. Guynemer gained nineteen of his fifty-four victories with this aircraft, which still exists.

Georges Guynemer in the deep cockpit of the first Spad 12 (S.382). Guynemer personally conducted much of the flight testing on the Spad 12. The bracket on the center-section struts was used to hold a camera. During testing, the aircraft carried the Stork insignia, but none of Guynemer's personal markings.

Guynemer Spad in flight

Guynemer victory over a Gotha-31st victory

Lt. Guynemer In His Plane

Spad VII S113 Guynemer flew

Victim of artillery 9-23-16

Hangar home of Spad VII S254

GuynemerSpad7 S254 after his death

GuynemerSpad7 S254 after his death with personal pic

Le « VIEUX CHARLES », de l'Escadrille des Cicognes, Avion de chasse « Spad » du Capitaine Guynemer, avec lequel il a abattu 19 Avions ennemis

Made in the USA
Charleston, SC
19 September 2012